ALL NEW LETTERS FROM A NUT

ALSO BY TED L. NANCY

Letters from a Nut

More Letters from a Nut

Extra Nutty! Even More
Letters from a Nut

Hello Junk Mail!

ALL NEW LETTERS FROM A NUT

TED L. NANCY

BROADWAY BOOKS
NEW YORK

For my parents, Rita and Marty Marder
So beautiful

FOREWORD

Here we stand on the precipice of an entirely fresh batch of brand new Ted L. Nancy Letters from a Nut. Conceived in lunacy, and released into wide circulation to the general public. And I feel the moment for me to finally reveal the truth that I possess about this mysterious man has arrived. The time has come for me to at last admit everything I know, and that I know everything.

In the 15 years that the Ted L. Nancy legend began there has been much circumspection about his identity, his whereabouts and his intentions. Many have claimed to be Ted Nancy, know Ted Nancy, write for Ted Nancy. Some have even guessed that I, Jerry Seinfeld, the two commercial spokesperson for the Microsoft Corporation, am the real Ted. All of these allegations, even the true ones, are false.

I have been asked so many questions.

"Who is this Nancy?"

"Why does he not come forward?"

"Why is he traveling with 300 hamsters to Amsterdam to put on a play called 'Hamsterdam'?"

"How is he able to reach the President of Latvia and then persuade his Excellency to consider being the head of Ted's 'Walnut Club'?"

"Why is Ted the only one to report that VONS Supermarket Black Cherry soda has the ability to send telekinetic messages?"

What about his other characters like Tiny Bennett and Small McCartney? Performers he insists are not midgets but "diminutives".

Is he really about to travel to Crete, Greece to perform his play, "Is Andy There?"? (Which was changed at the last minute to "Is Michael There?") And why must he rehearse the entire production in a hotel lobby?

Who are these other associates of his, Roy Gum, Don Gargle, Torry Hippo, Ralph Hem and Ben Gooey? Also Juanita Mincey and Boniva Rodriguez. What about the outdoor portable bathrooms called 'Pie Ala Commodes' and the Swanson Gastric Bypass TV Dinners?

Who is the true source of all these odd, yet oddly compelling ideas?

I can conceal the secret no longer. I can't live with myself. I don't know why I ever got involved with this. It all seemed so innocent at the beginning. A few letters, a little good natured fun. But now millions of books have been sold. The relentless drumbeat of public curiosity continues to mount.

Of course, I am directly responsible for encouraging this man in these activities year after year. I thought eventually the interest would wane and it would all just slowly disappear. But the opposite has happened. One Best Seller followed another, and then another. What is going on, I thought. Can there really be that many people silently rooting for Ted L. Nancy to succeed in opening up a restaurant next to "KOO KOO ROO Chicken" called "I Am The Walrus"?

I know now that there is only one way out of this very strange set of circumstances. I must unmask him publicly. I, Jerry Seinfeld, who at one time along with Bill Gates moved into the home of a normal American family telling them only, "I just want to live with you people." I will show the real Ted L. Nancy to the world on national television. And I will do it on the station that is "#1 for News".

And then the world will see, once and for all time, that just because someone claims to possess a moist towelette from the Civil War and wants it included in a Museum of other moist towelettes does not mean that we must all be dragged down into the Chickamauga.

Jerry Seinfeld

New York City

ALL NEW LETTERS FROM A NUT

VALSTS
KANCELEJA

Brīvības bulvāris 36, Rīga, LV-1520, Latvija
Tālr.: 67082934, fakss: 67280469
E-pasts: vk@mk.gov.lv
www.mk.gov.lv

Prioritaire
Prioritāra

i A M thA WEd

CA 91201

Nancy
Kenneth Rd # 193
dale

LATVIJAS
≡060
PASTS
260015

10

3A

1413 1/2 Kenneth Rd. #193
Glendale, CA 91201

Lost & Found
Bar Harbor Hotel
Newport Drive Bar Harbor,
Maine 04609 USA   14 Apr 2009

Dear Bar Harbor Hotel:

I am wondering if you found a pair of RUBBER GORILLA FEET that I
left in your mens room the evening of Thursday Apr 10. I was
visiting your restaurant that evening and used the restroom. i
was in town to give a performance at a birthday party for a Mr.
Juan and was in partial costume and, I believe, left my feet in
your hotel mens room.

I was probably distracted when I needed to use the tissue
dispenser and noticed it was empty, so I went to another stall to
get a handful of tissue and to see if you had a sani guard. With
both stalls open and me being disoriented I may have become
confused and distracted. These rubber feet are large as they are
gorilla feet, (lowland) size 15, with bunches of hair on them.
(they are rubbery) They have no value other than as part of a
costume I wear for birthday parties and events that I am in. i
probably left them behind when I used the bathroom. They may
still be in there.

Or perhaps another guest turned them in. you have a fine hotel
and are most courteous to your diners. I enjoyed my dinner there.

Respectfully,

Ted L. Nancy
Ted L. Nancy

P.S. You have great bread

14

Bar Harbor Inn
OCEANFRONT RESORT & SPA
NEWPORT DRIVE, BAR HARBOR, MAINE 04609
207-288-3351   800-248-3351
www.barharborinn.com

Dear Mr Nancy

I'm sorry to tell you we did not have any rubber zorilla feet turned in. Hope you found them.

Hsk dept
Elna Strout

TED L. NANCY
560 N. Moorpark Rd. #236
Thousand Oaks, CA 91360

Business Information
RED BLUFF CHAMBER OF COMMERCE
100 Main St.
Red Bluff, CA 96080

Dear Red Bluff Chamber Of Commerce:

I had written to you before and am still awaiting my answer. Can
you help me? Thank you. I have an act where I glue myself to
your bus bench. This is for your townspeople that have
accumulated 100 or more points in your semi calendar year. (will
take chits) .

Please assemble all your finest townspeople to a bus bench and I
will already be there glued to the bench for 52 straight hours.
They can look at me. DO NOT SNIFF THE AIR! I don't worry about
bathroom breaks. (need wooden type benches with slats in it)
Please only so much glue. My mind wanders after 3 tubes. Treat
me with respect as i am doing this for you!

This is no cheap glue stunt. This is no bummy gluing of myself to
your bus bench. I am the class of the gluing yourself to bus
bench acts. I am Gluey Vuitton. LARRY! (sorry I had a relapse
from a generic drug) Please have your entire town meet me in the
park. And no crunchy potato chip eating?

i need glue company and bus bench information. A list of all your
glue factories. And all bus benches. I will be arriving by
sleeping net.

Sincerely,

Ted L. Nancy
Ted L. Nancy

Red Bluff - Tehama County

Chamber of Commerce

P.O. Box 850
100 Main Street
Red Bluff, CA 96080
(530) 527-6220

e-mail: rbtccofc@tehama.net
www.redblufftehamacntyinfo.com

Ted L. Nancy
560 Moorpark Road #236
Thousand Oaks, CA 91360

Dear Ted:

      This is the first time we have heard from you! I am sorry, but we do not have bus benches (we are not big enough for mass transit)....nor do we have any glue manufacturers. We are enclosing some information about our area. Let us know if there is anything else we can help with!

Sincerely,

John Yingling, EVP
Red Bluff-Tehama County
Chamber of Commerce

JY/mt

Agriculture • Commerce • Industry • Recreation
Since 1876

TED L. NANCY
1413 1/2 Kenneth Rd. #193
Glendale, CA 91201   USA

Reservations
Amstel Hotel
Professor Tulpplein 1
1018 GX Amsterdam
The Netherlands   Mar 31, 2009

Dear Amstel Hotel:

Can you direct me to the proper office for assistance? I am
staging my play in Amsterdam and need to know what health permits
I need to stay at your hotel for 12 nights, May 16-27, 2009.

My play is called HAMSTERDAM. It involves a telling of your
beautiful city, a complete history, using hamsters. There are
over 300 hamsters I use in the performance. All hamsters have
been inoculated for any hamster diseases. I keep them contained
in special "hamster bins" which have been cleared by local U.S.
health peoples. I believe his name is Andy. (Have paperwork)
HAMSTERDAM is a tour of Amsterdam showing the beginning of your
city, which settled as a small fishing village in 1275. I use
real water but a fake fish. I cover the Dutch Golden Age using
real hamster food which is a mixture of crickets, pumpkin seeds,
& dry toast. In the performance I touch on the oldest building in
Amsterdam het Houten Huys. I will NOT mention your Red Light
District as my show is for seniors and frankly they are not
interested any more. However I do make one reference to "Miss
Lillian", a female hamster I have that is promiscuous. (but this
is tasteful) This is also cleared with Andy on all inoculations.

What permits do I need to bring 300 loose hamsters into your hotel
and have them live in the room with me. This is for 12 nights.
No animals will be hurt. I gave a Civil War reenactment with
Geese over 1200 times with no injury to the Geese. Although an
electrician was shocked and limp on a power line (but was revived
and driven home by his wife) I am hoping to interest Tarmo Mitt,
the worlds strongest man in this. Will let you know. Thank you
for your help. Your hotel is wonderful.

Sincerely,

Ted L. Nancy
Ted L. Nancy

INTERCONTINENTAL.
AMSTEL AMSTERDAM

Dear Ted,

Thank you very much for your letter.

Unfortunatly the hamsters are not aloud in our InterContinetal Amstel hotel. The InterContinental Amstel Hotel can not accomodate 300 hamsters in a room.

Please be assured that we hope that you're show will be a great event, but we can not reserve a room for the hamsters.

Please do not hesitate to contact us, if we can be of any further assistance.

With kind regards,

Oscar Vermeij
Reservations Trainee

on behalf of

Lotte Maas
Reservations Supervisor
INTERCONTINENTAL AMSTEL AMSTERDAM

Professor Tulpplein 1
1018 GX Amsterdam
The Netherlands
Phone: +31 (0)20 520 3176
Office fax: +31 (0)20 520 3181

For more information on Amsterdam's top attractions, best restaurants and in the know experiences, visit:

Prof. Tulpplein I, 1018 GX Amsterdam, Netherlands, Tel: +31 (0)20 622 6060, Fax: +31 (0)20 622 5808, amstel@ihg.com, www.intercontinental.com
This Hotel is owned by B.V. Amstel Hotel Maatschappij and operated by IHG Management (Netherlands) B.V.
ABN AMRO Bank, Amsterdam, Accountnr.: 43.56.31.187, IBAN: NL41ABNA0435631187, BIC: ABNANL2A
Chamber of Commerce Amsterdam: 34253641, VAT nr.: NL816156992B01

INTERCONTINENTAL.
AMSTEL AMSTERDAM

Bezoek ook
onze website:

www.ichotelsgroup.com

AMSTERDAM | ⊕ ⓉⓃⓉ | post

16.04.09 | € 00095 ct

Prof. Tulpplein 1 | # FR 816240
1018 GX | Nederland

TED L. NANCY
1413 ½ Kenneth Rd. #193
GGlendale, CA 91201
USA

TED L. NANCY
1413 1/2 Kenneth Rd. #193
Glendale, CA 91201   USA

Reservations
Amstel Hotel
Professor Tulpplein 1
1018 GX Amsterdam
The Netherlands   5/18/9

Dear Hotel Amstel Reservations:

Thank you very kindly for getting back to me. In this day and age
it is so nice to deal with a hotel as professional and dignified
as yours. I understand your concern about keeping 300 hamsters in
my room. It is wrong. I now realize that is a disease issue.

That is why I have decided to re-stage my HAMSTERDAM play. It is
now called: AMSTERCLAM. It will take place June 18-29 in your
city. It involves a telling of your Amsterdam using clams. I use
500 clams in the performance. All clams have been inoculated for
diseases. I keep them contained in special "clam cups" which have
been cleared by local U.S. health peoples. I believe his name is
Andy. (Have paperwork)

AMSTERCLAM is a telling of Amsterdam showing the beginning of your
city, which settled as a fishing village in 1275. I cover the
Dutch Golden Age using real clam food which is crickets, pumpkin
seeds, & dry toast. In the performance I touch on the oldest
building in Amsterdam het Houten Huys. I will NOT mention your
Red Light District as my show is for seniors.

Now. I need 3 rooms for 12 nights, June 18-29, 2009. I need to
bring 500 clams into your hotel and have them live in the rooms
with me. Clams are not like filthy hamsters. They are wet.
These clams will be kept all over the room on the bed and the
dressers & the rug glopping in their shells. They squish around.
They will undulate around the room. Please alert Housekeeping so
when they open the door they can spray. This is for 12 nights. I
was hoping to interest Tarmo Mitt, the worlds strongest man in
this. But he said "no." Thank you for your help. Your hotel is
wonderful. To reiterate: June 18-29, 12 nights, 3 rooms, 500
clams. Lysol spray. I look forward to my reply.

Sincerely,

Ted L. Nancy
Ted L. Nancy

The Hague, June 17, 2009

Mr. Ted L. Nancy
1413 ½ Kenneth Road No. 193
Glendale, CA 91201

Dear Mr. Nancy,

Thank you for your letter of March 31, 2009, in which you describe your play "Hamster-dam" and your inquiry about the requirements for bringing to the Netherlands your troupe of 300 performing hamsters.

The Netherlands is a member country of the European Union, which has harmonized regulations for the non-commercial importation of pets. The standard document for a pet is the so-called "pet passport." You can apply for pet passports at the nearest U.S. Passport agency office or selected U.S. Post Offices. The facility nearest you is the Glendale Main Post Office, 313 E Broadway, Glendale, CA 91209-9998, telephone 818-265-9200. You may download the passport application forms from the U.S. Department of State website. You should bring with you the completed and signed applications (inked paw-prints are acceptable) plus two 2-inch by 2-inch color photos of each hamster. These photos should be full-face frontal view, and the hamsters should be in their normal attire, not their costumes. Because the hamsters are under 16, they do not need to accompany you when you apply for their passports, but you will need to document that you are their legal guardian. The normal delivery time for a passport is 4 to 6 weeks; expedited service is available for a surcharge.

You and your hamsters do not require a visa to visit the Netherlands; they are eligible for the hamster visa waiver program.

An additional consideration is that the European Hamster, Cricetus cricetus, is indigenous to the Netherlands and is a protected species. Therefore, you will need to assure immigration authorities that your hamsters will not crossbreed with the Dutch hamsters. We note in particular that Miss Lillian may prove troublesome in this regard. You will need to provide documents from your veterinarian that each of the hamsters has been spayed or neutered, or has been on a recognized birth control regimen for 3 months prior to arrival, or has been trained in the use of condoms. If the latter, then you need to ensure that the hamsters have ready access to accepted condoms; hamster prophylactics are readily available in pharmacies and pet stores in the Netherlands.

You will also need to show immigration authorities that your hamsters have return tickets to the United States. Your failure to do so may lead these authorities to believe that your cast is part of a commercial shipment destined for pet shops or restaurants. In this case, Dutch immigration will require documentation that none of the hamsters is the product of genetic modification; European food laws are very strict concerning the approval of products of biotechnology for human food use.

The Embassy Community and I are very much looking forward to your presentation of "Hamsterdam." In this, the 400th anniversary year of Henry Hudson's historic voyage of discovery to the New York area, activities such as yours can go far to enhance the already strong bilateral relationship between the United States and the Netherlands. Please let us know if you need any financial assistance with your presentation. Our Public Diplomacy office has special funds that can be used to assist theatrical productions such as yours.

We look forward to your visit and to your successful performance, and I am certain Dutch and American expatriates will flock to see "Hamsterdam, The History of Amsterdam."

With best regards,

Michael F. Gallagher
Chargé d'affaires a.i.

1413 1/2 Kenneth Rd. #193
Glendale, CA 91201
f.d.nancy@lycos.com

Mall Leasing Information
Swire Properties Management Ltd.
Pacific Place Management Office
13/F One Pacific Place
88 Queensway Hong Kong   Apr 9, 2009

Dear Mall Leasing:

Can you please direct me to Mall leasing information for my store.

I own "NOT YOUR GRANDFATHER'S DIAPER OLD TYME ICE CREAM PARLOR". I
need to rent mall space in Hong Kong. We have an 1890's type olde
tyme ice cream parlor with a player piano and all our waiters are
seniors. We will hire locally. Speak to Alvin. He's in the
back. I have had many shoppes in Sweden that were successful and
now I open in USA. People love the "grandfatherly". Sweden is a
wonderful old tyme country.

Can you send me leasing information? A strip mall or lesser space
is fine. Does not have to be fancy. Just looking for space. We
will have approximately 32 employees: servers, kitchen help, ice
cream makers, jimmy loaders, maraschino cherry stem separators.
There will be 16 tables and a counter. But i could reverse this.

We have a large cardboard cutout in front of our "Grandfather".
Please tell me how I can protect this cutout; that it does not get
vandalized as teenagers throw food at it. I can adjust the outfit
in the cutout if you deem so. It is washable. Or I can put a
drape on the Grandfather. But it is our image and we like to be
true to our old tyme ice cream shoppe and our name. Can we chain
this cutout to a mall post? Once again, if needed, I can drape our
Grandfather. But why? People expect to see our servers as they
want them to look just like our cardboard cutout. That's our
attraction. Just like you see a Pirate outfit on a waiter in a
Captain's Seafood restaurant.

I look forward to hearing from you on Mall rental. Hong Kong is a
beautiful city. I once had meal there and it was enjoyable. You
come recommended. Call me Fred sometimes. People do.

Respectfully,

Fred D. Nancy
Fred D. Nancy
Ted

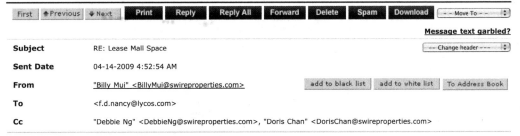

Message text garbled?

Subject	RE: Lease Mall Space
Sent Date	04-14-2009 4:52:54 AM
From	"Billy Mui" <BillyMui@swireproperties.com>
To	<f.d.nancy@lycos.com>
Cc	"Debbie Ng" <DebbieNg@swireproperties.com>, "Doris Chan" <DorisChan@swireproperties.com>

– – Change header – – |
add to black list | add to white list | To Address Book

Dear Fred

Thank you for your email on 10 April 09 and some information on "GRANDFATHER".

Regrettably, Pacific Place is fully let at the moment. Despite so, we do have plan to include your proposed trade and would be grateful if you could submit more of your company information for our review. Should there be change of plan in future and subitable opportunity coming up, we shall definitely be in contact with you.

We thank you for your interest again.

Best regards

Billy Mui
Swire Properties Management Limited
Pacific Place Management Office
Tel: 2844-8336
Fax: 2596-0616
billymui@swireproperties.com

1413 1/2 Kenneth Rd. #193
Glendale, CA 91201
f.d.nancy@lycos.com

Billy Mui
Pacific Place Management Office
13/F One Pacific Place
88 Queensway Hong Kong   15 Apr 09

Dear Mr. Billy Mui,

Thank you so kindly for getting back to me with mall leasing
information and calling me Fred. I sincerely appreciate it and
that is why your company comes so recommended. I know you said
Pacific Place Mall is full but you may have a plan to find me mall
space. I am interestd. I plan on leasing more then one space
over the next time period as my business is succeeding in other
areas.

I will now seek mall space for: "NOT WITH GRANDMA'S SPORTS BRA
YOU DON'T". This was an afternoon revue in German casinos and now
I want to open an eatery based on this revue. While the revue was
saucy in the casinos, my restaurant will be an old tyme waffle
shoppe with seniors as our waiters. (Just like in the revue). We
have an 1890's type waffle parlor with a velvet swing where our
Grandma swings over the diners. We will hire locally. Speak to
Maurio. He's in the back. We will have 14 employees: waitresses,
kitchen help, swing attendant, syrup sorter, butter padder. There
will be 16 tables and a counter. But i could reverse this.

We have a large cardboard cutout in front of our "Grandma".
Please tell me how I can protect this cutout; that it does not get
vandalized as teenagers threw food at it in front of the casino.
I can adjust the outfit in the cutout if you deem so. It is
washable. Or I can put a covering on the top of Grandmother. But
it is our image and we like to be true to our old tyme waffles and
our name. Can we chain this cutout to a kiosk? Once again, if
needed, I can drape Grandma on top. But why? People expect to
see our servers as they want them to look just like in our
cardboard cutout. That's our attraction. Just like you see a
Ballerina costume on a waitress in a Dancer's Restaurant.

I look forward to hearing from you on Mall rental. Hong Kong is a
beautiful country. I once had a fudgicle there and it was
enjoyable.

Thank you.

Fred D. Nancy

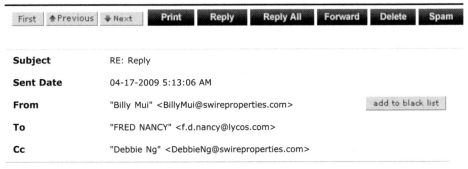

Subject	RE: Reply
Sent Date	04-17-2009 5:13:06 AM
From	"Billy Mui" <BillyMui@swireproperties.com>
To	"FRED NANCY" <f.d.nancy@lycos.com>
Cc	"Debbie Ng" <DebbieNg@swireproperties.com>

add to black list

Dear Fred

Thank you for your email again on 16 April 09.

Pacific Place is fully let at the moment and we do not project a space opportunity till end 2010. We shall advise you when a space becomes available.

We thank you for your interest again.

Best regards

Billy Mui
Swire Properties Management Limited
Pacific Place Management Office
Tel: 2844-8336
Fax: 2596-0616
billymui@swireproperties.com

                                        1413 1/2 Kenneth Rd. #193
                                        Glendale, CA 91201

Raffles Hotel Singapore
1 Beach Road Singapore 189673
Email: roomreservation@raffles.com   6 Apr 09

Dear Raffles Hotel:

You have been HIGHLY recommended to me by a Russian recommendation
list. Your hotel, I understand, caters to the traveler of which I
am one. I will be arriving by steamer trunk on the Cunnard and
need a room for 9 nights May 12-19 exiting on the morn. of the
20th and returning by sea plane. I travel w/ my companion Roy
Tonsil who looks like Lawrence Fishburne with Red Hair.

I will practice winking in my room. For a wink contest in your
city. I need wink shades & wink wipes. Can you supply or do I
have to go into the market square and buy them? Believe me I
will pay over retail just so I can have them in the room.

Please confirm:

Room reservation 9 nights May 12-19 Suite, please
Wink shades & wink wipes, possibly wink knobs

Like I said I am willing to pay over retail for the convenience of
having them in the room when I arrive so i can start winking.
(for contest.)   Wish me luck

Respectfully,

Ted L. Nancy

Enquiry (12-20 May) HOTELS

Raffles Hotel Room Reservations

Raffles Hotel Concierge   Apr 6

Tedlnancy1@gmail.com
Mon, Apr 6, 2009 at 10:58 PM
RE: Enquiry (12-20 May)

Dear Mr Nancy,

Greetings from the Concierge, Raffles Hotel.

Could you kindly advise as to what is a winking contesting so that we could
recommended/purchase the correct items.

Please do not hesitate to contact us should you require any further assistance.

Thank You

Kind Regards,

Fiona | Concierge | **Raffles Hotel Singapore** | DID: +65 6412 1180 | Fax: +65 6338 6885 | 1
Beach Road Singapore 189673 | Email: |
Web: | *E-brochure: http://www.raffles.com:81/EN_RA/Property/RHS/
LeftFooterNavigation/Media_Room/Gallery/eBooks/*

1413 1/2 Kenneth Rd.   #193
Glendale, CA 91201

Fiona Concierge
Raffles Hotel Singapore
1 Beach Road Singapore 189673
Email: roomreservation@raffles.com   7 Apr 2009

Dear Raffles Hotel Singapore,

Thank you for getting back to me so promptly. Like I said you
have been highly recommended and now i can see why. I will note
this promptness in my Raffles Folder and look at it when arrival
to remind me.

I may need 12 nights now. May 12-22 exiting on the morn. of the
23rd . There will be 3 of us, myself and Roy Tonsil, and another
gent. Do we need to get a bigger suite? 2 suites? Or a cot in
the room?

You asked in your letter: "Could you kindly advise as to what is
a winking contesting so that we could recommended/purchase the
correct items. Our Concierge colleagues will revert to you
shortly on your wink shades and wink pipe requirements".

I am in Singapore for the Wink Contest and need: Wink WIPES. NOT
a WINK PIPE which is for a different contest. I also need wink
knob, wink cloth. Can you arrange? (i will pay above market value
for convenience) in my room so I may start practicing for the
contest. I did not win last year and would like to reverse that.

Please advise as to ROOM(s) for 12 nights and new guest beside us
two and the wink supplies. Thank you for your excellent service
(which I will put in my folder).

Respectfully,

Ted L. Nancy

Exclusive Offers
Book Early at Raffles Hotel, Singapore

Enqiury (12-22 May)

Apr 8

TedInancy1@gmail.com
Raffles Hotel Concierge
<Concierge.RafflesHotel@raffles.com>
Wed, Apr 8, 2009 at 1:45 AM
Enqiury (12-22 May)

Dear Mr Nancy,

RE: Mr Nancy and Mr Roy Tonsil
ARR: 12 May 2009 (Flight to be advised)
DEP: 22 May 2009 (Flight to be advised)

General Enquiries   HOTELS X

Dear Mr Ted,

Greetings from the concierge desk at Raffles!

With regards to your enquiry for the place of purchase for WINK wipes and knobs, maybe know when and where exactly is the contest being held?
Please advice on this matter.
Thank you

Kind Regards,

Ash | Concierge| **Raffles Hotel Singapore** | DID: +65 6412 1180| Fax: +65 6338 6885| 1 Beach Road Singapore 189673 | Email: |
Web: | E-brochure:
http://www.raffles.com:81/EN_RA/Property/RHS/
LeftFooterNavigation/Media_Room/Gallery/eBooks/

1413 1/2 Kenneth Rd. #193
Glendale, CA 91201

Fiona Concierge
Raffles Hotel Singapore
1 Beach Road Singapore 189673
Email: room reservation@raffles.com   9 Apr 09

Dear Raffles Concierge

Thank you for answering me so we can get reservation paid for.
The new companions name is DON GARGLE. Please put him on all
correspondence as we are going to a foreign country and do not
need any stoppage of Mr. Gargle along the way.

Now. In answer to your question: "when and where exactly is the
contest being held?" We will meet at Esplanade Park. I believe
near the Tan Kim Seng Fountain. There's a foot path there. (i am
told) I am surprised you have never heard of Wink Contests which
are popular in the USA. Last year we held our contest in
Greenland, now in your beautiful city of Singapore. Raffles comes
highly recommended by coincidentally someone who sold us Wink
Wipes in Greenland. But has no ability to sell us in Singapore.
Can you get?

We will meet in the park for our PRE-meeting, hold our contest,
then all go back to my room for wink discussions and more winking.
that is why i need: WINK WIPES, WINK KNOBS. Blink pipes are for
blinking, not winking. Blinking is with 2 eyes, winking one eye.
if it rains we will all meet in my room. there will be 33 people
winking in room but not to stay. Or perhaps you can suggest hotel
conference room to rent. (only if it rains) Can we make
reservation ? I need to secure room for 13 nights for the three
of us.

We Do not want to stay in other hotel. Tell me what credit card
you need to secure reservation for 3 of us. I thank you once
again for your most courteous reply.

Respectfully,

Ted L. Nancy

Room Rservation   HOTELS X

TED L. NANCY
Raffles Hotel Concierge
TED L. NANCY ·   show details Apr 14   Reply

--------- Forwarded message ---------
From: Raffles Hotel Concierge <Concierge.RafflesHotel@raffles.com>
Date: Tue, 14 Apr 2009 13:24:48 +0800
Subject: RE: Room Rservation
To: "TED L. NANCY" <tedlnancy1@gmail.com>

Dear Mr Nancy,

Greetings from the Concierge, Raffles Hotel.

We do apologise that WINK is not played as popular in Singapore.
However we would love to assist you in getting the necessary items so
it would be great if you could kindly advise us on what is a WINK and
what exactly are the items and maybe a brief description so that we
could go source it out for you.

Please do not hesitate to contact us should you require any further
assistance.

Thank You

Kind Regards,

Fiona? Concierge? Raffles Hotel Singapore ? DID: +65 6412 1180?
Fax:
+65 6338 6885? 1 Beach Road Singapore 189673 ? Email:
concierge.raffleshotel@raffles.com? Web: http://www.raffleshotel.com

33

1413 1/2 Kenneth Rd.   #193
Glendale, CA 91201
tedlnancy1@gmail.com

Fiona Concierge
Raffles Hotel Singapore
1 Beach Road Singapore 189673   16 Apr 09
Concierge.RafflesHotel@raffles.com

Dear Raffles Hotel.

Sorry for the delay in answering you. I was organizing our club
and gearing up for my reservation with Raffles when one of our
members needed gauze attention. Can you please include Donald
Gargle on all correspondence as he is our Wink Leader and I show
him all bills. I am glad you now see how Popular Wink is in other
parts of the country. It is truly a sensation and a wonderful way
to communicate with others. We are happy to have Raffles getting
us rooms.

I now need: a BLINK Pipe after all. As the 2 clubs are combining
for this event. Blink is 2 eyes, wink 1 eye. but because the
economy is sour we are holding both clubs & meetings in Singapore
this year at the same time. There will be quite a few of us
dining & drinking in your restaurants & bars and then winking &
blinking back in the 2 suites. It will be grand. So. I need:

Many Blink Pipes (maybe 30 should be able to get in your market
place)
Blink Cloths (same amount)
NO wipes.

Time is getting close so we must make our reservations soon. What
do you need from me? I am ready.

Ted L. Nancy (MR)
Donald Gargle (MR)

P.S. what is Business Travel Mice China and TTG Mice magazine ?

560 No. Moorpark Rd. #236
Thousand Oaks, CA 91360 USA

President
COLOSSO WAFFLE CONES
Ace Baking Company
P.O.Box 2476
Green Bay, WI 54306

Dear Mr. Waffle Cone President,

I want to compliment your Colosso Danish Style Waffle Cones.
Recently I had the chance to use your waffle cone (not as
directed) and I can say I was cheerily pleased. On your product
is says:

"For generations the Danes have maintained their passion for
scrumptious treats. Colosso Waffle Cones bring the authentic,
just-baked taste of Danish waffles to you."

My family has long admired waffles. We come from a long line of
people that have admired waffles. I want to tell you: YOU HAVE
THE FINEST WAFFLE CONES I HAVE EVER TASTED!!! I AM PLOTZING HERE!
Yes, the Danish are phenomenal makers of treats. You ever get a
cup of coffee and a Danish? Where do you think the name came
from? The Danish. They're naming the whole country after a
snack. That is dedication to treats. Your entire staff should be
singled out. This is a team to be proud of. To make a waffle
cone like this. For me. To eat.

Please let me know everyone was thanked. I need that. It is
those of us out here in the non waffle cone world that appreciate
Stradivarius waffle craftsmanship you have. You make THE FINEST
WAFFLE CONE I HAVE EVER EATEN!!! I CAN'T TAKE IT ANYMORE!!! And
believe me, I eat waffle cones. (although not so much anymore
since my ankles gave out.) Let me know about the thanking.

With Respect For Waffle Cones,

Ted L. Nancy

America's Cone Experts™

Mr. Ted L. Nancy
560 N. Moorpark Road #236
Thousand Oaks, CA 91360

Dear Mr. Nancy,

We would like to take this opportunity to thank you for the words of praise and compliments on our "Colosso Danish Style Waffle Products". We are proud to be the manufacture of such a scrumptious treat.

Many customers have found very creative uses for our products other than for ice cream. We are excited to be a part of that creative experience.

As per your request we have posted your letter for all employees to receive your appreciate first hand. We are proud of our team and have received a rating of "Superior" from AIB (American Institute of Baking) to further verify that we are a top flight organization.

To show our appreciation for your compliments and team acknowledgment we are sending along a couple of Colosso coupons for your continued enjoyment.

Again, thank you.

Sincerely,

Judy Fogarty

Judy Fogarty
Sales Coordinator

ENC:

ACE BAKING COMPANY
Limited Partnership

1122 Lincoln Street ▼ P.O. Box 2476 ▼ Green Bay, WI 54306-2476
Tel: 414.497.7062 or 800.879.2231 ▼ Fax: 414.497.1893

1413 1/2 Kenneth Rd. #193
Glendale, CA 91201 USA

Prime Minister Valdis Dombrovskis
Brivibas Boulevard 36,
Riga, LV-1520
Latvia   12/11//2009

Dear MR. Prime Minister Valdis Dombrovskis of Latvia. .

Just a note to you to say what a great job you do for our world as
Prime Minister of Latvia, my birthplace and home for me during
April in the forest). It is outstanding the work you do and
should be noted.

I admire and what you have done for ALL Peoples. Not just for
members of our Latvian Club. We meet on Wednesdays; Jaseps
Ludvigs is our President. You are well regarded at our meetings
as we discuss all things Latvian including the food. (I like
bacon buns - Piragi!) Who doesn't like Sautéed Sauerkraut?

One of our club members was a laboratory assistant with you at
Mainz University. He currently makes keys. Another club member
said you both had an interest in physics and took pictures
together. He showed us one. He has a hat on with a feather in
it. If you like you could be the head of our walnut club.
Consider it. Post will be open until 3/12/2010. Then
Bendiks Mikelis will probably get it or maybe Kristaps Ludis. It
is a small peaceful world.

Thank you for you reply. Keep up the good work.

PLEASE SEND ME A PICTURE. I will show it to my Latvian club .
(then put it away)

With utter respect,

F.D. Nancy

COMMUNICATION DEPARTMENT

36 Brīvības Blvd., Rīga, LV-1520, Latvia, Phone: + 371 67082828, Fax: + 371 67284450
E-mail: prese@mk.gov.lv, www.mk.gov.lv

Rīga

No.88/N-62

Januar 11, 2010

F.D.Nancy
1413 1/2 Kenneth Rd # 193
Glendale
CA 91201
USA

Dear *Mr. Nancy,*

Thank you for your letter. The State Chancellery of the Republic of Latvia appreciates and values people of foreign countries showing interest about Latvia. It is also nice that you are informed about the members of our Government and especially about Valdis Dombrovskis, Prime Minister of the Republic of Latvia.

Prime Minister of the Republic of Latvia Valdis Dombrovskis, born on August 5, 1971, has become the youngest head of the Latvian Government. In his career, V.Dombrovskis has been a Member of the 8th *Saeima* (Parliament) of the Republic of Latvia, the Minister for Finance, and in July 2004, as a representative of the "New Era" Party, was elected to the European Parliament.

The Prime Minister V.Dombrovskis had earned a Master's degree in Physics and from 1997 till 1998 studied in the doctoral programme at the Department of Electrical Engineering of the University of Maryland.

Please, find enclosed a photo of the Prime Minister with his autograph.

You can find out more about our Government in the Internet home page of the Cabinet of Ministers. Its address is: **www.mk.gov.lv/en** .

We wish you good luck!

Sincerely,

Aivis Freidenfelds
Press secretary of the Cabinet of Ministers

560 No. Moorpark Rd. #236
Thousand Oaks, CA 91360   USA

CUSTOMER SATISFACTION DEPT.
VONS SUPERMARKETS
P.O. Box 3338
Los Angeles, CA 90051

Dear Vons Supermarkets,

I am writing to you with a problem I am having with your VONS DIET
BLACK CHERRY SODA. It is the first time I have ever tried this
brand. I believe this soda is sending me telekinetic messages.
It is bad. The can communicates with me. I spilled some soda on
my kitchen floor. There was a face in the spill. It winked at
me. What is that about, Vons?

Your Diet Root Beer is fine, no weird activity. I believe this
black cherry soda is trying to communicate with me. From the
grave. It is evil, Vons. It has a face on it. Is that possible?
I enjoy your Diet Cola.

I have had problems before with a haunted sponge from Ralphs. I
locked it up in my basement with 1,000 nails. but it got out and
stayed by my bed. It looked at me. Although to date I have not
had any further experiences with paranormal cleaning equipment.

I am scared, Vons. What can i do? Do you sell Mop and Glo?

Respectfully,

Ted L. Nancy

the
VONS.
Companies, Inc.

Ted L. Nancy
560 N. Moorpark Rd., #216
Thousand Oaks, CA 91360

Dear Mr. Nancy:

Thank you for writing to us regarding Vons Select diet Black Cherry Soda. We take great pride in our products, and we appreciate knowing when there is a problem.

As you know, Vons guarantees the products it sells because we believe our store brands are as good or better than the national brands and want our customers to know that they can get a refund or replacement if they are not satisfied.

Thank you for shopping with us. I am enclosing a gift certificate to reimburse you for the product what was not satisfactory.

Sincerely,

Dotti Baker

Dotti Baker
Consumer Affairs Representative

DWB:dvm

Enc.

cc: W. Kovac

The Vons Companies, Inc. • P.O. Box 3338, Los Angeles, CA 90051-1338
618 Michillinda Avenue, Arcadia, CA 91007-6300 • Telephone: (818) 821-7000

Harriet Carter ® GIFTS, INC.

425 STUMP ROAD
NORTH WALES, PA 19454

9120131421 CC08

i hAVE miSSED
you

Rd. #193

1201

02 1M
0004223287
MAILED FROM ZIP CODE 18936

UNITED STATES POSTAGE
PITNEY BOWES
$ 00.44°
JUL 24 2009

1413 1/2 Kenneth Rd. #193
Glendale, CA 91201
tedlnancy1@gmail.com

Room Reservations
Mandarin Oriental Hotel
211 Nihonbashi Muromachi
Chuo-ku, Tokyo 103-8328, Japan   6 Aug 2009
motyo-reservations@mohg.com

Dear Hotel reservations.

I will be arriving by aircage for the PAPER HAT CONVENTION in your
city, Sep 22-Sep 30, 2009 I will need a room for those nights. A
suite please as myself and my companion LAWRENCE GUM will be
arriving together. Mr Gum has special needs. Can they be
accommodated? Your hotel is highly recommended by paper hat
workers at the San Rafael Plant.

I understand the Mandarin Oriental Hotel offers guests soup in
their rooms. I would like that. Let's get Lawrence Gum some
soup. I have been in paper hats since 1981. There is exciting
new developments in paper hats. Incl. air mesh and non stick
bands. Plus complete paper uniforms. We are just working on the
tearing now. I love this field and all the exciting challenges.
Can you recommend any place in town for me to do anything?

To recap: I need room for 9 nights Sep 22-30 for myself and Mr.
Gum. How can we proceed? Your Tapas Molecular Bar and use of
syringes are recommended by Japan peoples.

Thank you,

Ted L. Nancy

Room Reservations Inbox x

TED L. NANCY

MOTYO -
Reservations

"TED L. NANCY"
<tedlnancy1@gmail.com>
Thu, Aug 6, 2009 at
10:09 PM
[Mandarin Oriental,
Tokyo] RE: Room
Reservations

10:09 PM (23 minutes ago)

Dear Ms. Ted,

Warm greetings from Mandarin Oriental, Tokyo!

Thank you very much for your email and inquiry for your accommodation in Tokyo.

We are delighted to offer our Mandarin Suite either King or Twin at special rate of JPY89,000.
Please note that rates above are subject to 10% service charge, 5% consumption tax and 200 Japanese Yen per person.

Regarding special needs for Mr. Gum, we do have soaps as well as shower gel as room amenity.
For your inquiry about activities, our concierge will get back to you directly.

Our Tapas Molecular Bar is one of the most recommended place to enjoy dinner as showing on TV and magazines.
Since advanced reservation is required, kindly refer available dates and time listed below.
If you wish to make a reservation, please let us know your preferred date and time.
Please note the availability is as of today.

We hope this special offer is acceptable to you.
We look forward to hearing from you soon.

Warm regards,

Miwa Muto (Ms)
Room Reservations

address   2-1-1 Nihonbashi Muromachi

             Chuo-ku, Tokyo 103-8328 Japan

telephone   +81 (3) 3270 8950

facsimile   +81 (3) 3270 8886

email

website

1413 1/2 Kenneth Rd. #193
Glendale, CA 91201
tedlnancy1@gmail.com

Room Reservations
Mandarin Oriental Hotel
211 Nihonbashi Muromachi
Chuo-ku, Tokyo 103-8328, Japan   8 Aug 2009
motyo-reservations@mohg.com

Dear hotel Reservations

Thank you for your prompt answer to me. It is delightful to deal
with such professionals as yourself. Now. Down to my
reservations.

Mr. Gum needs soup in his room. Not soap. Although chicken
noodle soap sounds dee-licious. Can you get in my room? (or
minestrone soap if you are out of chicken noodle soap)

What room in the hotel is holding the Paper Hat Convention? If
it's not there let me know. I still need to stay at your hotel as
it is close to my waffle cone business. I will wear paper 3 piece
suit.

To recap: I need room for 9 nights Sep 22-30 for myself and Mr.
Gum. A deluxe suite, please. How can we proceed? Your
professionalism is most appreciated. I think we are ready to get
confirmation. How?

Respectfully,

Ted L. Nancy

Room Reservations   Inbox   X

TED L. NANCY

MOTYO - Reservations

TED L. NANCY

TED L. NANCY

TED L. NANCY

MOTYO - Reservations   9:17 PM (1 hour ago)

"TED L. NANCY"
<tedlnancy1@gmail.com>
Sun, Aug 9, 2009 at 9:17 PM
[Mandarin Oriental, Tokyo]
RE: Room Reservations

Dear Ms. Ted,

Thank you very much for your reply.
We apologize for the delay in replying as our Sales department is closed over
the weekend.

After we checked with our Sales department, we do not have any functions for
the Paper Hat Convention during that period.
We are sorry that we are not able to locate the function although I have tried to
find.

Regarding the soup, I am really sorry that I misunderstood the word carelessly.
We do not have a chicken noodle soup as a regular menu, however, we are
delighted to prepare it if the order is made one week in advance.
The price for a chicken noodle soup is JPY1,500 plus 10% service charge and
we can also prepare a minestrone soup as well at price of JPY1,200 plus 10%
service charge.
Kindly advise us delivery time for the chicken noodle soup for Mr. Gum and if it is
for daily arrangement.

For your room type, kindly advise us if we should go ahead and book a Mandarin
Suite room at JPY89,000 which we offered previously.
Once your room type and bed type (king or twin) are confirmed and we received
your credit card information to secure your booking, we will email your
confirmation letter immediately.

Should you have any further questions or concerns, please feel free to contact
us.

We look forward to hearing from you soon.

Warm regards,

Miwa Muto (Ms)
Room Reservations

 MANDARIN ORIENTAL
TOKYO

address   2-1-1 Nihonbashi Muromachi

1413 1/2 Kenneth Rd. #193
Glendale, CA 91201
tedlnancy1@gmail.com

Room Reservations
Mandarin Oriental Hotel
211 Nihonbashi Muromachi
Chuo-ku, Tokyo 103-8328, Japan   10 Aug 2009
motyo-reservations@mohg.com

Dear Mandarin Oriental Hotel Reservations .

Thank you once again for your wonderful detail to customer
service. It is truly a delight to deal with such professionals as
yourselves. Just magnificent. It will be noted in my folder and
shown to others.

As I mentioned, Mr. Gum has special needs. Can he get chicken
noodle SOAP? In his room? Or if you are out of chicken noodle,
then minestrone SOAP will do. We will pay premium for this.
(more then JPY 1,500 and more then 10% service fee; maybe 12%)
Please call me Fred or Fred D. Or F.D. from time to time.

I await my reply.

Respectfully,

Ted L. Nancy
(F. D. Nancy)

46

RE: Sightseeing recommenations, convention HOTELS X

MOTYO - Concierge to me   Aug 10 (4 days ago)

Dear Mr Nancy

Attached please find sightseeing recommendations for Tokyo. I hope you find this useful.

By the way, we checked with the major convention centers in the city but were unable to find a Paper Hat Convention. Do you know the name of the center where this convention is to be held?

Sincerely

Adam Chapin

Concierge

Mandarin Oriental, Tokyo

MANDARIN ORIENTAL
TOKYO

address   2-1-1 Nihonbashi Muromachi
           Chuo-ku, Tokyo 103-8328, Japan

telephone +81 (3) 3270 8800

facsimile +81 (3) 3270 8828

email

1413 1/2 Kenneth Rd. #193
Glendale, CA 91201
tedlnancy1@gmail.com

Room Reservations
Mandarin Oriental Hotel
211 Nihonbashi Muromachi
Chuo-ku, Tokyo 103-8328, Japan   14 Aug 2009
motyo-reservations@mohg.com

Dear Mandarin Oriental Hotel Reservations .

Thank you once more for your exceptional regard to hotel
amenities. It will be noted & stapled in my folder. (and three
hole punched) It is truly wonderful to deal with professionals as
yourselves. Just splendid.

Now. Let us address Mr. Lawrence Gum and his needs. Mr. Gum is
the Chair Committee Chief of the Paper Hat Convention. He
oversees 3,000 people in paper hats. He will be in my room. So.
Just to make sure what we are talking about here regarding the
Chicken Noodle SOAP. I am assuming this is the soap you wash in
the shower with that has chicken, noodles, carrots, and possibly
celery in it. It depends on how you make it. The minestrone SOAP
is made with vegetables, pasta, beans, onions, and tomatoes. Low
salt please. Then Mr. Gum will be washed up and fed with the same
bar of soap.

And ready to enter your lobby with his paper hat on to command
3,000 others in paper clothing. We have still not figured out the
tearing. Sorrreee. Please, look away when someone crosses their
legs. You ask: "Do you know the name of the center where this
convention is to be held?" Yes. I believe it is at The Mandarin
Oriental Hotel. How far away is that?

How do we proceed? When can we finalize? What is next?

Sincerely,

Ted L. Nancy
(Fred)

Room Reservations

MOTYO - Reservations <motyo-reservations@mohg.com> Fri, Aug 14, 2009 at 6:50 PM
To: "TED L. NANCY" <tedlnancy1@gmail.com>

Dear Ms. Ted,

Thank you very much for your reply.

In order to arrange a chicken noodle soup in your room for Mr. Gum, we would like to reserve your room first. We await your preferred bed type and credit card information to guarantee your booking.

We look forward to hearing from you.

Warm regards,

Reiko Watanabe (Ms)
Room Reservations

address	2-1-1 Nihonbashi Muromachi Chuo-ku, Tokyo 103-8328, Japan
telephone	+81 (3) 3270 8950
facsimile	+81 (3) 3270 8886
email	motyo-reservations@mohg.com
website	http://www.mandarinoriental.com/tokyo/

Make an entrance,

1413 1/2 Kenneth Rd. #193
Glendale, CA 91201
tedlnancy1@gmail.com

Room Reservations
Mandarin Oriental Hotel
211 Nihonbashi Muromachi
Chuo-ku, Tokyo 103-8328, Japan   15 Aug 2009
motyo-reservations@mohg.com

Dear Mandarin Oriental Hotel Reservations .

Again. Thank you for your distinguished attention to hotel
elegancies. It will be noted & glued in my folder.

Now. Lawrence Gum has lost the Chair Committee Presidency and is
being replaced by RICHARD MOUTH who has requested Split Pea SOAP
in the shower. Can you make? Or if you are out of Split Pea then
Navy Bean SOAP. Please no Gazpacho. He does not like cold
showers or cold soup. Heavy salt please.

Mr. Mouth will lead the 5600 members in your lobby, all in paper
clothing. He may not wear a paper hat. He has a red thing on his
head. (the heartbreak of psoriasis) Mr. Mouth will be staying an
additional 4 nights so 13 nights for us. Your finest
accommodations.

Just so we know what we request. Mr. Mouth will step into the
shower. put Split Pea SOAP on himself and wash. You ask Bed
type. Rye or whole wheat is fine.

what is next? I look forward to the Paper Hat Convention in your
hotel. Still working on the paper clothing tearing. PLEASE! No
water sprayed on us. Look away when we bend.

Respectfully,

Ted L. Nancy
Ted L. Nancy

F.D. NANCY (MR)
1413 1/2 Kenneth Rd. #193
Glendale, CA 91201   USA

Licenses
CITY OF HUNTINGTON BEACH
2000 Main Street
1st St.
Huntington Beach, CA 92648   5, April 2009

Dear City Of Huntington Beach:

I am moving to Huntington Beach soon with my ELECTRONIC NOSE
BLOWING MACHINE. I will keep this machine on my patio. How far
do I have to be from another apartment when this machine
activates? It is part of my noise study Thesis for my degree. I
am involved in the study of apartment noises and how they affect
others.

What licenses do i need?

My Nose Blowing machine makes a loud noise as if someone is
blowing their nose without a tissue. In my studies this is
annoying. The machine activates about 12 times per day. Every 2
hours for about 9 "blows." Some short, 2 long, some louder then
others, some muffled. This varies. At 3 in the morning, the
noise gets a little louder. I do throw in a ringer noise, which
is not nose blowing but an animal grunt noise, just to see if the
person living in the next apartment can distinguish between a
human and an animal on my patio.

The machine electronically mixes up the blow sounds so sometimes
it is 4 short noises, sometimes one really long one, yet other
times, a series of sharp "honks." This will be the final study
for me for my degree.

Thank you for your help. I look forward to living in Huntington
Beach with my Electronic Nose Machine.

Please send me license information for this machine.

Respectfully,

F. D. Nancy
F.D. Nancy

Certificate of Occupancy No. O200

APPLICATION FOR CERTIFICATE OF OCCUPANCY
CITY OF HUNTINGTON BEACH – DEPT. OF BUILDING & SAFETY

(3rd Floor – Must Apply In-Person)

714/536-5271

Business License # _____   Date **4/2009**

Business Address _____   Zip Code _____

Business Owners Name **TED L. NANcy**   Telephone No. _____

Business Name _____   Bus. Phone _____

Business Type **Nose Blowing Machine**

Property Owner Information *(required)*	Tenant/Emergency Contact *(required)*
Name _____	Name _____
Address _____	Home Address _____
City _____ State/Zip _____	City _____ State/Zip _____
Telephone No. _____	Telephone No. _____

THIS USE WOULD BE DESCRIBED AS:
   ☐ Newly Constructed Building   or   ☐ Existing Building

CHECK ALL THAT APPLY:
   ☐ Change of Property Owner   ☐ Change of Occupant   ☐ Change of Use   ☐ Additional Occupant
- Indicate former type of business _____
- Are you requesting that the electricity be turned on? Yes☐No☐
- **Is the building sprinklered? Yes ☑No☐**
- Will operations produce dust/wood shavings or similar material? Yes☑No☐
- Will operations involve the repair or replacement of automobile parts Yes ☑No ☐   If yes: Describe the components repaired or replaced. **TIRE RIM**
- Does the operation involve the use of welding or open flame? Yes ☑No ☐
- Will the business be a drinking, dining or assembly use with an occupant load of more than 50 persons? Yes ☐No ☐
- The following best describes my operation: ☐ Office Only ☐ Retail Sales   ☐ Medical/Dental
   ☐ Restaurant/Take Out Food   ☐ Warehouse /Manufacturing/Distribution
   (describe process and end product) _____
   ☑ Other (describe) **Blow My Nose on People**

☐ Will the facility have any of the following equipment?   Yes ☑No ☐
   Charbroiler
   Dry cleaning machine
   Spray Booth
   Printing Press (screen/lithographic/flexographic)
   Internal combustion engine (greater than 50HP) (excluding motor vehicles)
   Boiler/combustion equipment (greater than 2 million BTU/hr. maximum in-
   Abrasive blasting cabinet/room
   Baghouse/cartridge type dust filter/scrubber
   Motor fuel storage and dispensing equipment

☐ Will any of the following operations be performed?
   Application of paints or adhesives
   Etching, plating, casting, or melting of metals
   Molding and blending of liquids and/or powders
   Storage of acids, solvents, organic liquids or fuels
   Production of acids, solvents, organic liquids, or fuels
   Production of fumes, dust, smoke or strong odors

No.STRIL. Spray

RETURN SERVICE

CITY of HUNTINGTON BEACH
P.O. Box 190
Huntington Beach, CA 92648-2702

$00.39¢
US POSTAGE

F.D. Nancy
14134 Kenneth Rd #193
Glendale CA 91201

52

1413 1/2 Kenneth Rd. #193
Glendale, CA 91201

Customer Relations:
LOAF N JUG CONVENIENCE STORES
Kroeger
1014 Vine Street
Cincinnati, Ohio 45202-1100   11/19/2009

Dear Loaf N Jug Customer peoples,

I shop almost exclusively at Loaf N Jug. For me the convenience
is much needed, I eat donuts, burritos, Snackwells from your
local store in Colorodo where i live most of the time. I read
magazines in the aisle and am very happy with the courteous
service you show to me. Your Sloshee is refreshing!

I was at a Loaf N Jug and noticed a cardboard cutout. It was near
the pretzels. It gets jostled over there. This cutout deserves a
better life. I can give it that. I like the pictures of people
on the cutouts. They are seniors. The clerk told me you had all
the pictures and to contact you at loaf n lug

Can you assist me with buying this cutout and these pictures? I
really just need the faces. To show others. I can haul it away
myself. I will put a hat on it.

Please let me know how i purchase this cutout from your store.

Thank you,

Ted L. Nancy

Ted L. Nancy

The Kroger Co. ♦ 1014 Vine Street ♦ Cincinnati, Ohio 45202-1100

November 25, 2009

Mr. Ted L. Nancy
1413 1/2 W Kenneth Rd # 193
Glendale, CA 91201-1478

Dear Mr. Nancy:

Thank you for writing to us regarding a cutout or prop hat you wish to purchase that is on display at one of our Loaf 'N Jug stores.

Please let us know which store you see the display. Also, the Store Manager may be able to assist you with a quick answer for your request. Our Store Manager may have to make a call to the Corporate Loaf N Jug Office located in Pueblo, CO for more information.

Thank you again for contacting us. Our Product Information Line toll free number is: 1-800-632-6900.

Sincerely,

Ellen Griffin

Ellen Griffin
Consumer Response Representative
Ref. # 7425884

1413 1/2 Kenneth Rd. #193
Glendale, CA 91201

Customer Service
Harriet Carter Gifts,
425 Stump Road,
North Wales, PA. 19454.   Jul 14, 2009

Dear Harriet Carter Gifts,

I want to order a product from you. My ELECTRONIC NOSE BLOWING
MACHINE blew out. My neighbor attacked it. He listened to it all
night and then at 3 in the morning came after it with a machete.
He became viscious with it. I think it over-blew. It was
supposed to blow its nose 12 times during the night, every 40
minutes. It reversed and blew its nose 40 times in 12 minutes.
He then jumped over the fence and attacked it. I need a new one.

Can I order another nose blowing machine from you? Thank you,
Harriet Carter, for being a company that carries these products.
We all need assistance.

Is Shelly there?

Sincerely,

Ted L. Nancy

Thank you for your inquiry. I am sending information about the Neti Pot. It is not electronic though.

Thank you.

7/23/09

Harriet Carter Gifts
Customer Service Dept.
425 Stump Road
North Wales, PA 19454

Item: 9631

Click to view larger   Email: _____   [Send Email]

NETI POT INSTRUCTIONS   9631

1. Mix saline solution using 8 ounces WARM water and a heaping ¼ tsp. finely ground non-iodized salt, or ½ tsp coarsely ground salt. Fill the neti pot with the solution.
2. Tilt your head to one side and gently insert the spout of the neti pot into the upper nostril creating a seal between the neti pot and nostril. If the water drains into your mouth, keep you chin tucked down slightly. RELAX. If you are calm, the water flows right through. If you are tense, the water won't flow. Stay relaxed and breathe through your mouth. The saline solution should flow through the nose on its own. There is no forcing it.
3. Raise the neti pot slowly to develop a steady flow of saline solution through the upper nostril and out the lower nostril.
4. KEEP BREATHING THROUGH YOUR MOUTH .
5. When done, exhale firmly several times to clear the nasal passages.
6. Mix another batch of saline solution, tilt your head to the other side, and repeat the process.
7. When finished, rinse neti pot with clear warm water and dry inside and out.

The neti pot is plastic and made in China.

PPRDirect, Inc.
Brooklyn, NY 11232

C9631 - NETI POT $7.98

Catalog: 39 Page: 066

Stop nasal congestion fast for easy breathing all day, all night! 100% all-natural Neti Pot nasal cleaner unblocks clogged sinuses caused by colds, flu, allergy and chronic sinusitis. Centuries-old Indian treatment uses salt and warm water inside the "genie-like" lamp to irrigate each nasal passage for immediate, long-lasting relief. Eases the effects of pollen, dust, pollution and other irritants simply and easily. 7½" L.

1413 1/2 Kenneth Rd. #193
Glendale, CA 91201

Customer Service
Harriet Carter Gifts,
425 Stump Road,
North Wales, PA. 19454.   Aug 3, 2009

Dear Harriet Carter

Thank you for answering me regarding my Electronic Nose Blowing
Machine. When I wrote you in July and told you my neighbor ruined
my nose blowing machine by trashing it you were kind enough to
suggest another type of nose machine. This one had the picture of
the woman with the fireplace squeezer in her nostril. It worked!
Thank you Harriet Carter!

Now I am looking for an ELECTRONIC THROAT CLEARING MACHINE. For
snoring. Something with some sort of attachment that helps with
the snore symptoms in your throat.   Can you help?

Also. Do you have Stain Sleep Caps as I have heard? I look
forward to continuing to do business with you, a company that
helps its customers with their problems.

Respectfully,

Ted L. Nancy

PLEASE EXCUSE OUR INFORMALITY.
By using this note we are able to give you an immediate answer. We feel this is more important than sending a formal reply which could take several days.

Thank you for your interest in our mail 8/17/09 order catalog.

We are sorry to report that we do not carry the Electronic Throat Clearing Machine. However, we still carry the Satin Sleep Caps!

We have included order form and envelope for your convenience.

Harriet Carter Gifts
Customer Service Dept.
425 Stump Road
North Wales, PA 19454

Harriet Carter®
Distinctive Gifts Since 1958

A

A

Harriet Carter   Bed & Bath   Bath Accessories   Satin Sleep Cap

Satin Sleep Cap

Satin sleep cap keeps every hair in place, all night long, no matter how much you toss and turn! Jumbo cap fits over the fullest bouffant style, glides smoothly on the pillow, and stays in place with a non-binding elasticized band. Inner lining is made of breathable fabric for cool comfort. Washable poly/satin. Imported.

Satin Cap (Pink) (R8100)	~~$4.98~~	This item is unavailable.
Satin Cap (White) (B8101)	$4.98	0
Satin Cap (Blue) (B8102)	$4.98	0

1413 1/2 Kenneth Rd. #193
Glendale, CA 91201

Customer Service
Harriet Carter Gifts,
425 Stump Road,
North Wales, PA. 19454.   Aug 21, 2009

Dear Harriet Carter Gifts,

Thank you for writing me back regarding your Electronic Throat
Clearing Machine and Satin Sleep Cap. It's a wonderful item!

Now I want to know if you have the ELECTRIC CHAIR. · This is the
chair that is designed to shock those peoples that need
punishment. It is a wooden chair that you are strapped into. A
wet spongy leather cap is placed on your head (after shaving your
head & leg) Can i use the Satin Sleep Cap? Then the Harriet
Carter volt lever is pulled & 2,000 volts go through the offender.
Some mess may occur. Do you carry this item?   And maybe an
Electric End Table to go with it?

Also do you have Toe Socks as others have told me?

Harriet Carter is the finest co. out there for these kinds of
items. I tell many about you and your dedication to helping your
customers. At times I need to be addressed as F.D. Nancy.
Sometimes Fred. But now F.D.

Sincerely,

Ted L. Nancy
Ted L. Nancy
(F.D. Nancy)

Harriet Carter Gifts, Inc.
425 Stump Road
North Wales, PA 19454
215-361-5122

08/27/2009

Order Number: 0

MR F D NANCY
#193
1413 1/2 KENNETH RD
GLENDALE, CA 91201

Dear MR F D NANCY,

 Thank you for your letter and inquiry.

We do not carry the Electric Chair. But we do carry Toe Socks (please see enclosed picture).

Thank you for your kind words about our company. It is a pleasure to serve you.

Sincerely Yours,

HARRIET CARTER GIFTS

B9842 - TOE SEP SOCKS

Catalog: 39 Page: 023

6.98 a pair

Toe-separating socks keep your piggies apart, dry and healthy. Just slip on these soft, comfy open-toe socks for relief from a variety of toe and foot problems. They gently separate toes to help keep medicine in place, absorb moisture, prevent athlete's foot, blisters and corns. Made of machine-washable cotton/spandex. One size fits most. One pair. Imported.

1413 1/2 Kenneth Rd. #193
Glendale, CA 91201

Customer Service
Harriet Carter Gifts,
425 Stump Road,
North Wales, PA. 19454.   Sep 2, 2009

Dear Harriet Carter Gifts,

Thank you for answering me regarding the Electric Chair. I am
sorry you do not carry it.

Now. I was wondering if you carry the GAS CHAMBER. This is the
compartment designed to gas those peoples that need punishment.
Harriet Carter cyanide pellets are plopped into the compartment .
The curtain is then opened allowing the witnesses to observe the
punishee. A Harriet Carter lever is pulled and the poison gas is
sucked in through the nostrils. Responses can include convulsions
and excessive drooling. Do you carry this?

Also do you have DOG VESTS?

Harriet Carter is the best company i have ever heard of for
customer service, customer dedication, and general customer (need
another word here) I will note it in my folder.

Respectfully,

Ted L. Nancy
Ted L. Nancy

We do not carry the "Gas Chamber" or any pest repellant with your description

Harriet Carter Gifts
Customer Service Dept.
425 Stump Road
North Wales, PA 19454

The item is still available. Our item number and price is: (small)

B8173 (small)	Reflective Dog Vest	9.98
B8174 (med)	"	"
B8175 (large)	"	"

We have included order form and envelope for your convenience. Thank you for writing to Harriet Carter.

Harriet Carter Gifts
PO Box 2400
North Wales PA 19454-0911

1413 1/2 Kenneth Rd. #193
Glendale, CA 91201

Customer Service
Harriet Carter Gifts,
425 Stump Road,
North Wales, PA. 19454.   Nov 21, 2009

Dear Harriet Carter Gifts,

Thank you for answering me regarding my last letter on my Gas
Chamber item. I am sorry you do not carry it.

Now. I was wondering if you carry the SOLITARY CONFINEMENT CELL.
This is the Harriet Carter Adjustment Cell for those offenders
that need punishment in a Secured Housing Unit with no human
contact. Includes the Harriet Carter metal bed bolted to the wall
and the Harriet Carter metal toilet. The offender is locked down
23 hours a day, only allowed 1 hr outside his cell for Harriet
Carter exercise. He is fed only Harriet Carter Bread & Water.
Also can be used as a Pet carrier. Do you carry this?

Also do you have the SMART MOP? It soaks up ten times its weight
in water.

Harriet Carter is the best company i have ever heard of for
dedicated and devoted customer service, customer devotedness, and
allegiance (customer) & answering customer letters. I will note
it in my folder. (and show others)

Respectfully,

Ted L. Nancy
Ted L. Nancy

Harriet Carter Gifts, Inc.
425 Stump Road
North Wales, PA 19454
215-361-5122

11/25/2009

Order Number: 0

MR F D NANCY
193
1413 1/2 KENNETH RD
GLENDALE, CA 91201

Dear MR F D NANCY,

 Thank you for your inquiries about some products.

We do not carry the Solitary Confinement Cell for pet carrying. We do sell the Smart Mop (see enclosed picture).

Thank you.

Sincerely Yours,

HARRIET CARTER GIFTS

Harriet Carter
Distinctive Gifts Since 1958

Harriet Carter   As Seen on TV   Smart Mop®

Smart Mop® (F2267

Smart Mop® soaks up ten t
sponge or string mop—the s
any wet or dry mess in seco
wringing a simple, "no wet h
on any surface without swee
washable; lasts for years. Ir

- $14.98
- 2 for $28.50

1413 1/2 Kenneth Rd. #193
Glendale, CA 91201
TEDLNANCY1@GMAIL.COM

Enrollment
KAPLAN UNIVERSITY
6301 Kaplan University Avenue
Fort Lauderdale, FL 33309   5 Apr 09

Dear Kaplan University:

Please send me information on retraining myself through your
school. I have recently been laid off and seek a new education
for a new job.

I am an out of work quip writer for pillows. I worked in the quip
sector making up mottos and quips that were stitched onto pillows.
At one time this was a lucrative field. However with the economy
so down it is hard to get people to believe that a pillow with a
happy motto like: "EACH MORNING YOU WAKE UP AND YOU'LL BE UP" will
boost them. No one's paying $99.00 for a pillow with a motto on
it anymore. I used to work regularly as there were over 1000 quip
pillow stores in malls. I came up with the motto: "THAT DRIPPING
SOUND YOU HEAR IS YOUR BRAIN LEAKING GOOD THOUGHTS TO YOU" (that
was mine) This was stitched on over 1100 pillows and all sold.
(in good times) I even had one for the diabetic person who lost
part of his foot. "BE AN OPTIMIST. LOOK AT THE SHOE HALF FULL"
That did not sell. I read in Ohio one person smothered his wife
with a quip pillow. That shook me. (My motto on pillow)
Now I am seeking a new field to retrain myself as I now realize
after 34 years of this it was B.S. (to put it bluntly)

That's why I want to get my degree in Homeland Security. Let's
get me in there and starting securing peoples. Remember: "GET OUT
OF BED. ONCE YOU'RE UP YOU'RE UP". I am ready for a new career.

Send me information to take these classes. Thank you.

Respectfully,

Ted L. Nancy
"YOU'RE GOING TO LIKE THE WAY YOU LOOK. I GUARANTEE IT" (George
Zimmer the Mens Wearhouse)

May 6, 2009

Dear TED L.,

Congratulations on taking the first step toward reaching your career goals!

My name is Danial Riehle and I am your Kaplan Continuing Education Admissions Advisor. I have received your request for information regarding our Cisco Certified Design Professional. I have been trying to reach you, but the contact information I have must not be current or correct.

Please let me know how to contact you and the best time to reach you. I would like very much to talk to you about Kaplan's convenient online certificate program and how it can help you prepare for career success. Of course, you don't have to wait for my call. You can contact me anytime.

When we talk, I'll give you all the details about your course of study, costs, tuition assistance, books and software requirements. I'll also help you get started on the admissions process.

I'm looking forward to speaking with you soon and helping you take the next step on the road to professional success.

Thank you,

Danial Riehle
Admissions Advisor

Kaplan Continuing Education
6301 Kaplan University Avenue
Fort Lauderdale, FL 33309 USA

India: 000-800-650-1541
Hong Kong: 800-963-729
Jordan: Access code 18-800-000, Dial 888-833-4661
Philippines: 1-800-1-651-0534
Saudi Arabia: 800-844-4322
Singapore: 800-181-1102
Thailand: 001-800-656-975
UAE: 800-01-441-6296
Ext: 92003481

All other Email: KCEInternational@kaplan.edu

Accelerate Your Career Opportunity. Exceed Your Expections.

F.D. NANCY (MR)
1413 1/2 Kenneth Rd. #193
Glendale, CA 91201

Sessions Online School of Design
350 7th Ave, 2 floor
NY, NY 10001   4/8/9

Dear Sessions school:

I want to inquire about taking courses and learning a new career.
You have been recommended to me by others in my field who have
retrained with you.

I need to retrain! I am wasting my time in the PAPER HAT INDUSTRY
which is going under. No one has job anymore and even less want to
wear a paper hat. Boy what a waste of my last 37 years. Can you
help me? Now they are working on a paper uniform. How stupid is
that? The thing keeps tearing and showing everyone's underwear
and socks. They'll never get paper not to tear.

Someone told me there was a Taz there that was very good.

I was thinking of the PHOTOSHOP industry. Everybody photoshops
Let me work with them for $. I want to take your course. Please
write me with information.

I am ready to take all courses now in PHOTOSHOP or other course
you can recommend in your fine school.

My home address at top. email is: f.d.nancy@lycos.com

Sincerely.

F. D. Narcy

F.D. Nancy (MR)

Subject	Sessions - Admissions	- - Change header - - - ⏏
Sent Date	04-08-2009 5:41:40 PM	
From	Kerri Besse -- Sessions Online <Kerri@sessions.edu>	add to black list add to white list To Address Book
To	"F.d. Nancy" <f.d.nancy@lycos.com>	

Hi F.d. ,

Thank you for your interest in Sessions Online Schools of Art and Design.

Our Certificate Programs include: Graphic Design, Web Design, Multimedia, Digital Arts, and Marketing Design. The programs are extensive in that they provide you with the solid foundation and skills that you will need to succeed. There are three Certificate Program levels: Foundation, Advanced, and Master's.

The first step to getting started with your design courses is to complete our short application process. There is no fee for submitting your application to us. It is simply so we can begin to work together to find a program that best fits your goals, both career wise and financially.

So what is your dream job and which design Certificate program do you think will best suit your goals? I am a trained designer with over three years of freelance and full time design experience here in New York City. I am here to help you with your decision process as well as to answer your questions about our school!

Kind Regards,

Kerri

Kerri Besse,
Director of Admissions

F.D. NANCY (MR)
1413 1/2 Kenneth Rd. #193
Glendale, CA 91201
f.d.nancy@lycos.com

Sessions Online School of Design

Kerri Besse,
Director of Admissions
350 7th Avenue, 12th Floor
New York, NY 10001   Apr 15, 2009

Dear Kerri Besse,

Funny you and I both have last "first names" .   Now. Yes thank
you for checking in.   It is diligence like this that i certainly
appreciate in these times of "people not caring". you care and it
is noted in my folder.

Now down to my retraining. I have decided not to retrain in the
photoshop industry. I looked at a catalog of another school and
to tell you the truth it look photoshopped. I became sick. what
is real anymore?

I do need guidance though as I am a downsized waffle maker in an
old tyme waffle shoppe in a mall . Woo. that was one bad job.
sorting butter pads all day while teenagers vandalized the
cardboard cutout outside the store throwing food at it.

Do you offer classes in: FIGURE DRAWING?

There seems to be quite a few jobs I have seen advertised for
people to draw figures for very good money. How can i get in?
How do we work together? So what is the next step? Thank you for
getting back to me with figures so that I may draw.

Sincerely,

F.D. Nancy (Mr)

69

•; Print   Reply   Reply All   Forward   Delete | Spam   Download   Move To

Subject   Sessions – Admissions

Sent Date   04-16-2009 3:16:51 PM

From   Kern Besse – Sessions Online <Kerri@sessions.edu>

First I *Previous I *Next

To   "F.d. Nancy" <f.d.nancy@lycos.com>   **Message text garbled?**

Hi F.d.   -- Change header

Thank you for your reply and sharing your current goals. We do in fact offer a course in Figure Drawing and I do agree that it is best to assess only the courses that interest you the most. This course is being offered through our school of Fine Arts. Here is the direct link to this course:
http://finearts.sessions.edu/page2.asp?page_id=100027

I have taken this course myself. It was extremely helpful! The total cost for the course is $380.00 and it is 6 lessons in total. A 6 lesson course takes about 30 hours to complete.

Once you have had a chance to review the course information, you can feel free to e-mail the founder of the Fine Arts school, Jordon Schranz for more information. His e-mail is jordon@sessions.edu.

I am your Admissions Advisor and I am here to assist you with questions regarding tuition and course enrollments.

                                Best,

                                Kerri

Kern Besse,
Director of Admissions
Sessions Online@ Schools of Art & Design
800-258-4115 ext. 119
212-239-3080 ext. 119
Chat:
http://www.sessions.e
du/chat/

Sessions Online. @ Preparing
Design Professionals.
http://www.sessions.edu/portal
350 7th Avenue, 12th Floor
New York, NY 10001

F.D. NANCY (MR)
1413 1/2 Kenneth Rd. #193
Glendale, CA 91201
f.d.nancy@lycos.com

Sessions Online School of Design
Kerri Besse, Director of Admissions
350 7th Avenue, 12th Floor
New York, NY 10001   2 May 09

Dear Session School, Ms Besse

I am sorry i have not been back to you sooner. I was in the
hospital with a ladder accident.

Now down to my schooling: I wonder if i can make a living with
this figure drawing. I see a man every day drawing faces in front
of Vons supermarket and his shoes are worn and his tip cup is
empty. (& dirty) I stare at him and wonder. Is that me? So..

I would really like to make up quips that you can embroider onto
pillows. That is a field that is white hot. Can you tell me
about these classes? I think the field of coming up with mottos
and sayings and putting them onto pillows is the way to go. There
is a lot of these stores in malls.

do you have any courses in that? I know you have art courses and
design and graphics. How can you help me ? What can we do to get
me:

1. Into your school
2. In the art field?

Please call me Fred. It is Fred D. Nancy. Sessions has a
wonderful reputation for helping students tailor a field and
courses around what they can do. Can you help me?

Respectfully,

Fred Nancy
Fred Nancy

First I *Previous I *Next

Subject	RE: Taking Classes
Sent Date	05-04-2009 7:05:36 PM
From	"Jordon Schranz" <jordon@sessions.edu>
To	"Kerri Besse" <Kerri@sessions.edu>, <f.d.nancy@lycos.com>

Hi Fred,

My name is Jordon Schranz. I am the Director of Fine Arts for Sessions. I can answer any questions you may have in regards to our courses as well careers in the Art world.

I can tell you that doing the type of embroidery work you are referring to requires a high level of technical skill. That skill comes from both your ability to draw as well as your training with the equipment.

I can tell you that if you are interested in a career in the arts a strong foundation in drawing will be required. And don't worry, there are more jobs that that of street portrait artist (which is akin to there being more work in the field of music then playing in the subways).

Through your sessions courses you will be developing both the technical skills required as well as developing a portfolio that you will be able to use to gain work in fine arts and design.

If you have specific questions about enrollment you can contact admissions@sessions.edu. Otherwise, if you have any questions regarding our courses please contact me personally.

Thank you for your time and interest.

Jordon Schranz
Director of Fine Arts
Sessions School of Fine Arts
jordon@sessions.edu
http://finearts.sessions.edu

JACKSONVILLE UNIVERSITY

2800 University Boulevard N

Jacksonville, Florida 32211-3

ADMISSIONS

C-SM011 91201

is that SMELL
on your shoe
OR mine?

F. D. NANCY (MR)
1413 1/2 Kenneth Rd. #193
Glendale, CA 91201
f.d.nancy@lycos.com

Ordering dept.
SBICCA Shoes
2312 Edwards Ave.
South El Monte, Ca. 91733
store@sbiccashoes.com   22 Apr 09

Dear SBICCA Shoes,

I am in the process of opening BA-NANNYS in 16 malls. This is
NANNY WEAR that is bright yellow like a banana. It has caught on
in Finland where I have outfitted many Nannys.

Now I need to buy bright yellow shoes. Can you help me? Perhaps
you can suggest a design or style. I would be open to a meshy
shoe with a print on them. I have heard about your co. in prof.
meetings as one who is approved by the govt. I am open to your
suggestions. As long as these Nanny shoes are really yellow like
a banana. Could be some green on top like the stem.

I need to order many shoes in all sizes. We have a bright yellow
Nanny outfit and now I want to complete that with yellow banana
shoes. The yellow should be the color of a banana with a Banana
and a Nanny on the logo. I have a design to show you if you'd
like to see. You will know that a Nanny is in the room when she
is dressed from head to toe in bright yellow. It is very
comforting. You go, "Oh, it must be the Nanny." Just like you
notice bananas in a produce section. I have gotten many
commendations from Finnish authorities on this comfort.

Your company was mentioned as a fine USA co. I look forward to
your help and possibly the selling to me of bright yellow banana
shoes for my BA-NANNY company.

Respectfully,

F.D. Nancy

F.D. Nancy (MR)

Subject   Re: Ordering Shoes For My Business

Sent Date   04-22-2009 1:22:02 PM

From   "Sean Sbicca" <seansbicca@yahoo.com>

To   "FRED NANCY" <f.d.nancy@lycos.com>

Hello,

Could you send us an example of what your thinking of?

Thank you,
Sean Sbicca

F. D. NANCY (MR)
1413 1/2 Kenneth Rd. #193
Glendale, CA 91201

Mr. Sean Sbicca.
SBICCA Shoes
2312 Edwards Ave.
South El Monte, Ca. 91733   23 Apr 2009

Dear Mr. Sbicca,

Thank you for getting back to me on my BA-NANNY SHOES.

I have enclosed drawings for you of the BANANNY SHOE. They are
bright yellow and look like a banana. They will compliment my
bright yellow Bananny uniform, easy to spot when a Nanny wears it.
This is very comforting to others.

However, I am open to your designs too. As long as the shoe is
comfortable and easy to wear. Should be spongy underneath and
cushiony inside.

Let me know what you think Your company is highly recommended by
Finnish produce peoples. I have heard of Sbacca in my dealings in
Finland. However, Nannys are currently wearing other shoes then
mine BUT with my Nanny clothing. That should change with these
shoes. I need to order many.

Respectfully,

F.D. Nancy

F.D. Nancy (MR)

BA·NANNY Shoe Drawings

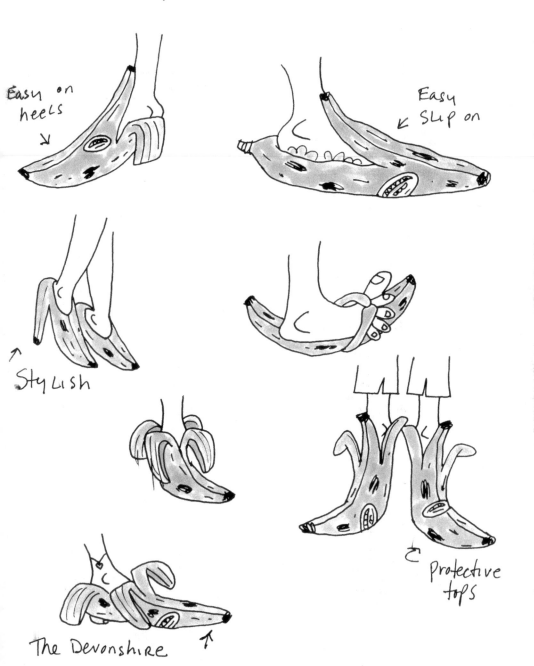

Easy on heels

Easy ← Slip on

↑ Stylish

↳ Protective tops

The Devonshire ↑

7075 COMMERCE CIRCLE SUITE C
PLEASANTON CA 94588
PHONE: 925-469-9111
FAX: 925-469-9112
BELVEDERESHOES.COM

BELVEDERE INC

Fax

To: _F.D. NANCY_ From: _RICHARD_

Fax: _____ Pages: _1_

Phone: _____ Date: _4-22-09_

Re: _____ cc: _____

☐ Urgent ☐ For Review ☐ Please Comment ☐ Please Reply ☐ Please Recycle

• Comments:

MR. NANCY: GOOD LUCK WITH "NANNY WEAR"
I CAN BE OF NO HELP WITH YELLOW COLOR
SHOES FOR THE CLOTHING. I DID NOT ANSWER
BY E-MAIL BECAUSE OF ALL THE PROBLEMS WITH
COMPUTER VIRUS, BUT I WANTED TO LET YOU
KNOW I DID RECEIVE THE E-MAIL SORRY
I CAN'T BE OF ANY HELP.

SINCERLY
R. TOBASCO
BELVEDERE SHOES

F. D. NANCY (MR)
1413 1/2 Kenneth Rd. #193
Glendale, CA 91201
f.d.nancy@lycos.com

MR. TOBASCO
BELVEDERE SHOES
7075 Commerce Circle Suite C
Pleasanton, CA 94588   27 Apr 09

Dear MR. TOBASCO:

Thank you for getting back to me on my BA-NANNY shoes. I
appreciate you can not make yellow shoes. However I am in need of
another shoe for my food service industry clothing.

I own WAITER-MELONS. This is uniforms for the Waiter industry
that are bright red with black seeds on them like a watermelon.
Waitermelons are popular in Denmark where it is a joy to be able
to spot your waiter in a restaurant by my brightly colored
uniform. I am proud of the service i bring to diners. And have
been commandended by the Danish restaurant Industry which is
notorious for poor service. (Platinum Gold Circle award) Now
diners can see their waiters easily in my clothing.

I now need shoes for these uniforms. Bright red shoes with black
seeds on them. (possibly some green like the rind but am open)
Can you make?

I enclose my Waitermelon designs for you. I have certificates from
the Danish Business Community. I was referred to you to make me
large amounts of shoes.   The referral came from the garment
indus. at prof. meetings. When can we speak? How do we do this?
I am open to designs as long as the shoes are:

Bright red
Black seeds on them
Look like watermelons

I look forward to hearing from you, Mr. Tobasco. Thank you, sir.

Respectfully,

F.D. Nancy

Watter-Melons Shoes

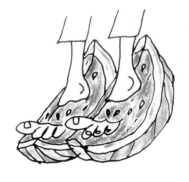

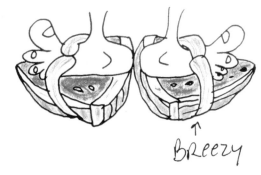

BReezy

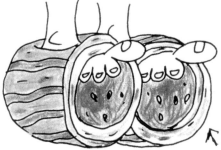

The CONQuistadoR

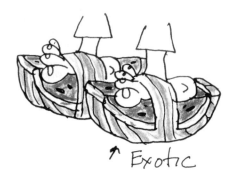

Exotic

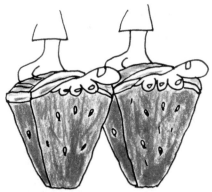

Fashionable

Sturdy

TED L. NANCY
1413 1/2 Kenneth Rd. #193
Glendale, CA 91201
TEDLNANCY1@gmail.com

Sales Assistance
Satellite Industries Toilets
2530 Xenium Lane N.
Minneapolis, MN 55441-3695   May 24, 2009

Dear Satellite Industries Toilets

I am in need of many Portable Toilets. And want to order from
you.

Soon I will open PAPA'S JOHNS. This is a COMMODE company, a porta
potty business supplying commodes to fairs, flea markets, etc. We
have supplied porta pottys in the past to Arturo's Mite Carnival &
Lice Capades. Some lice was lost in one of the commodes never to
be retrieved.

We get our name from the term "Papa" and we have a DAD on our
logo. As in "PAPA'S JOHNS. We are not affiliated with PAPA JOHNS
PIZZA. They are food and I am waste.

We use seniors to work. Seniors like the opportunity to be busy
and work outdoors and we are happy to employ them locally.
Although they wander off. We ask them to wear orange traffic
vests.

Can you send me information on the kinds of commodes and other
toilet products I can order from you? We need many.
You have been recommended. Papa Johns has fine pizza. I yummed
some up recently.

Respectfully,

Ted L. Nancy
owner PAPA'S JOHNS COMMODES

RE: Satellite Quote Request

9 messages

Ron Sprenger <RonS@satelliteco.com>   Tue, May 26, 2009 at 5:33 AM
To: "TED L. NANCY" <TEDLNANCY1@gmail.com>

Ted,

Thank you for the request for information on our restrooms.

Could you answer a couple questions so I can get you the right prices with shipping?

Do you want us to assembled these 100 Maxims at your location or do you need these delivered already assembled or do you plan on assembling the restrooms yourself.

What color are you looking for?

Will 91201 zip code be the final shipping location?

On the 200 Breeze---do you need foaming soap or liquid soap dispenser?

Also do you prefer single fold or multi fold paper towel dispensers?

Thank you,

Ron   1-800-272-3280

Satellite Industries Portable Toilet and Restroom manufacturer, vacuum service trucks/tanks, deodorizers, handwash units and other accessories for portable toilets.

TED L. NANCY
1413 1/2 Kenneth Rd. #193
Glendale, CA 91201
TEDLNANCY1@gmail.com

Ron Sprenger
Satellite Industries Toilets
2530 Xenium Lane N.
Minneapolis, MN 55441-3695   June 3, 2009

Dear Mr. Ron Sprenger,

Thank you for getting back to me regarding portable toilets for my
business: PAPA'S JOHNS COMMODES. I am sorry i am tardy in
returning your correspondence but i have been in the process of
changing our name from Papa's Johns Commodes to: ELTON'S JOHNS.
People were confusing the pizza with my waste business. Bad for
both of us. But this new name will not have any confusion.

Re: your request. YES! Please assemble 1000 commodes. (How much
more for this?) You ask what color. Brown. I also need foaming
soap as you mention. Am i leaving anything out? Please let me
know.   I look forward to your reply.

Respectfully,

Ted L. Nancy
owner ELTON'S JOHNS

RE: Satellite Quote Request

Ron Sprenger <RonS@satelliteco.com>
To: "TED L. NANCY" <tedlnancy1@gmail.com>

Wed, Jun 3, 2009 at 4:17 PM

Ted,

To have 100 Maxims delivered to your zip 91201 in Glendale, CA the price for each sand Maxim3000 with assembly included would be $516.00 and $2371.40 for shipping the entire load.

For each load of 104 Breeze hand wash units the price with (foaming & multi fold) dispensers is $462.00 each plus $2848.86.

Let me know what you decide.

Thanks   Ron   1-800-272-3280

TED L. NANCY
1413 1/2 Kenneth Rd. #193
Glendale, CA 91201
TEDLNANCY1@gmail.com

Ron Sprenger
Satellite Industries Toilets
2530 Xenium Lane N.
Minneapolis, MN 55441-3695   June 18, 2009

Dear Mr. Ron Sprenger,

Thank you for getting back to me regarding portable toilets for my
business: ELTON'S JOHNS. I am sorry i am tardy in returning your
correspondence. I have been Zebra teasing in New Guinea and lost
the tips of my fingers. Now. Down to business.

Once again i have had to change the name of my business. It is no
longer Elton's Johns. Something about a singer out there. So now
please address all correspondence to: NINCOMPOOPS

Let's talk toilets!

Re: your request. I need 1,000 Maxims. How much? And 1104
Breeze Hand Wash units. And yes with foaming and multi fold.
What color foam? I look forward to your reply.

Respectfully,

Ted L. Nancy
owner NINCOMPOOPS

RE: Satellite Quote Request SATELLITE COMMODES

Ron Sprenger

TED L. NANCY

TED L. NANCY

TED L. NANCY

Ron Sprenger

TED L. NANCY

Ron Sprenger   Jun 19
"TED L. NANCY" <tedlnancy1@gmail.com>
Fri, Jun 19, 2009 at 11:17 AM
RE: Satellite Quote Request

Ted,

You had asked for 100 Maxims and 200 Breeze units orginally.   Now you are asking for 1000 Maxims and 1104 Breeze. What is the correct amount?

Is Glendale the final shipping address?

This product would need to be paid for by bank wire transfer before shipment.

Will need these questions answered before we can move forward.

Thank you,

Ron

1413 1/2 Kenneth Rd. #193
Glendale, CA 91201

Donations Dept.
THE UNIVERSITY OF NORTH DAKOTA
University Relations
409 Twamley Hall
264 Centennial Dr. Stop 7144
Grand Forks, ND 58202   Aug 12, 2009

Dear The University of North Dakota :

I am writing to your fine college today with great honor for me.
I would like to leave a donation to The University of North
Dakota . Grand Forks holds a lot of fond memories and your school
has educated many. I have had 12 of your former students working
for me at various times.

I would like to now leave a donation to you. We are doing well.
Your past students have helped our business become what it is
today.

Who do I contact to leave my gift? Can you advise me? I am
honored to be able to do this. I look forward to your reply.

Sincerely,

F.D. Nancy

F.D. Nancy

FOUNDATION

3100 University Ave. Stop 8157 | 800.543.8764 / 701.777.2611
Grand Forks, ND 58202-8157 | fax: 701.777.4054

August 19, 2009

F.D. Nancy
1413 ½ Kenneth Rd. # 193
Glendale, CA 91201

Dear Mr. Nancy,

Greetings from everyone at the University of North Dakota! The fall semester begins next week, so the campus is very busy as students return and begin moving into the residence halls. This is always an exciting time on campus!

Mr. Nancy, thank you so much for your very kind letter. I am pleased to know that UND graduates have served you and your company so well. You mentioned you have fond memories of Grand Forks and UND. Did you grow up in Grand Forks? Or perhaps attend UND?

The University of North Dakota Foundation is the officially designation organization to receive gifts for the benefit of the University of North Dakota. We are a 501-c-3 organization which means we will issue a receipt to substantiate your gift for income tax charitable deduction purposes. We also ensure the funds donated are used to the exact specifications of the donor.

Enclosed is a bit of information about the UND Foundation and its mission to support the University of North Dakota. I have also enclosed a postage-paid return envelope for your convenience should you wish to make a cash gift. If you have questions about making a gift of stock or real estate, I will be happy to answer them. I can be reached at 1-800-543-8764.

Thank you again for what you are planning to do for the University of North Dakota. Kind regards.

Sincerely,

Deb Wilson, CGPA
Development Officer

Enclosures

1413 1/2 Kenneth Rd. #193
Glendale, CA 91201

Deb Wilson.
UNIVERSITY OF NORTH DAKOTA
3100 University Ave. Stop 8157
Grand Forks, ND 58202   Nov 18, 2009

Dear Ms. Deb Wilson, University Of North Dakota:

Thank you for writing back to me. Please excuse the tardiness in
answering you. I was behind a heavy person at a vending machine
and detained. Now. I am thrilled to leave you a donation.
Currently I own HUMPTY DUMPTYS porta potty commode company. We
supply portable toilets to Icelandic carnivals, Mid Pacific Rim
tattoo events, Guadalajara bullfights . We were formerly known as
PIE-ALA-COMMODES.

We are doing well. We used over 1 million Breeze Hand Washes in
the last 3 decades. (foaming & multi fold) We almost invented
Cabana Spray, & Graffiti Remover. (But we did not) Your past
students have helped our business become what it is today. As i
said I have had 12 of your former students working for me at
various times. One has a degree from your school. One student
works in our Moist Towelette Department. He has a cork in his
head. Another mows my lawn.

Now for my donation to your school: How does 1104 Breeze Hand
Wash Units sound? With foam. I am honored to do this. I will
have them assembled and shipped to Glendale and then you can pick
them up. How far is North Dakota? (May donate 1000 Maxims
Flushers too - they're the 3000's; don't know yet) I will also
give you some multi fold dispensers. (foamy - what color would
you like?) Go Hockey! I am still considering this donation.
Will let you know positively. (there's a lot of stuff here)

With respect,

F.D. Nancy (Ted L. Nancy)
F.D. Nancy (Ted L. Nancy)

TED L. NANCY
1413 1/2 Kenneth Rd. #193
Glendale, CA 91201
TEDLNANCY1@gmail.com

Customer Dept.
1 800 Vending
VENDING Support Team
1284 West Flint Meadow Drive
Kaysville, UT 84037   7/10/2009

Dear 1.800.VENDING COMPANY Peoples:

I am interested in owning VENDING MACHINES. I will sell Pajama
Bottoms from a vending machine at the airport. CARLO! Please
excuse me I blurt out Spanish mens names when my medication has
worn off. ANTONIO! I believe that people will buy pajama bottoms
at the airport. Why wouldn't they? Huh?   When can i get as much
information as you can send me on this vending stuff? I once ate
a 12 year old cracker from a vending machine   The filling was hard
but it still tasted like a cracker. I belched up a wrapper.

It's always nice to confer with those in the business world that
have good ideas. I once sold Kiosks from a vending machine. I
closed 7 hours into the next day.

Please reply with vending machine info. I will buy vending
machines from you. I look forward to it.

Respectfully,

Ted L. Nancy
Fred D.

Vending Company Comparison Chart VENDING x

Marty Lloyd
tedlnancy1@gmail.com
Fri, Jul 10, 2009 at 3:01 PM
Vending Company Comparison Chart

hide details **Jul 10**   Reply

Ted,
I have attached the Vending Comparison Chart I mentioned when we spoke on the phone and I made mention of it in the other email I already sent you.

I think you'll find this to be a good tool as you compare companies. The top portion of the chart – the Critical Factors – will help steer you away from unethical or questionable companies. The long term, reputable companies will all pass the Critical Factors test and then you can concentrate on machine features, support etc.

We've listed as many third party resources as possible so that you can do an independent analysis. Let me know if you have a hard time finding information on a particular company and I will see if our research department can supply a link to the information you are seeking.

I look forward to talking with you soon.

Marty Lloyd | Regional Manager| 1.800.VENDING
1284 West Flint Meadow Drive | Kaysville, UT 84037
☎: 1.800.836.3464, ext. 226 | ⮸: 1.801.593.6449
✉: marty@1800vending.com | www.1800vending.com

1413 1/2 Kenneth Rd. #193
Glendale, CA 91201

Marty Lloyd Regional Manager
1.800.VENDING COMPANY
1284 West Flint Meadow Drive
Kaysville, Utah 84037   Jul 10, 2009

Dear Marty Lloyd, Regional Manager, 1.800.VENDING:

Thank you for your emails. I read them when I watch Ice Truckers.
Soon the A & E Network will have Ham Munchers. This is high
octane extreme ham sandwich eating. Now. When did we talk on the
phone? Down to my vending machine needs. I will sell pictures of
Zac Efron's gums from a vending machine at the train station.
RAYON! Please excuse me I blurt out fabrics when i Twitter.
DENIM! I believe people will buy Zac Efron's gums from the train
station. Why wouldn't they? Huh?

Please load me up with as much information as you can on vending.
I CAN'T GET ENOUGH! I thought i could get enough. But I can't.
I once ate a 31 year old peanut log from a vending machine in
Daytona. The log itself was hard but it still tasted like a
peanut. I JUST MADE 2 ORBITS AROUND THE EARTH WITH GENE CERNAN!!!
(we ate vending machine tuna)

It's always nice to confer with those in the business world with
acumen. The professionalism you have shown will be noted and put
on a plaque and shown to Otto Doll. Do you carry the Maxims
Breeze Vending Machines? With foaming soap? Also do you prefer
single fold or multi fold paper towel dispensers?

Please reply with vending machine info. I look forward to it. i
can take more vending info. I have not had enough yet.

Respectfully,

Ted L. Nancy
Fred Nancy

1·800 VENDING®

Hi Ted,

Thank you for your interest in our 1.800.VENDING Refreshment Center, the highest-quality, most-versatile, and best-designed combo vending machine available, and for your interest in our company, where you get lifetime, unlimited, post-sale support and assistance to help ensure your success and satisfaction for years and years and decades to come. I missed speaking with you today. You will really love this. You can click on the attachment to see more about the 1.800.VENDING Refreshment Center and our vending distributorship startup program.

You can click on the attachment to see our current pricing information. This unique promotion was scheduled to end on June 30 but has been extended through July 20, and carries a lifetime price lock in addition to discount pricing, and that lower price even includes locations; it is unique in that it combines 3 promotions (discount pricing, locations included, and lifetime price lock) all simultaneously so this is very, very significant. You will love our machine and you will love working with our company.

If you have not already done so, I highly recommend that you visit http://www.1800vending.com where our Web site will show you *"The 3 Things You Need To Know Before Giving Any Vending Company A Dime"*.

I would also be happy to answer any questions you might have. You can reach me at 1.800.VENDING (1.800.836.3464) or on my direct line below.

Review these emails, call those locating specialists, and call me with any/all questions (about us or any other company or machine out there).

I look forward to speaking with you again soon.

Marty Lloyd | Regional Manager | 1.800.VENDING
1284 West Flint Meadow Drive | Kaysville, UT 84037
☎ : 801.953.0400 direct | 📠 : 801.593.6449 fax
✉: marty@1800vending.com | www.1800vending.com

```
                              F. D. NANCY
                              1413 1/2 Kenneth Rd. #193
                              Glendale, CA 91201




University Marketing & Communications
Jacksonville University
2800 University Blvd North
Jacksonville, FL 32211                4, Apr 09



Dear Jacsonville University:

I am confirming my appearance at your University for Saturday May
30, 2009.  In my documentation from you I was told to contact you
6 weeks before to arrange particulars.  A quality motel is fine as
long as smoking and baking is available in my room.  Syracuse
University is a fine school.  Coincidentally my neighbor's friend
who drives an ice cream truck graduated from there.

So you may set up my appearance, my act is:  I am LORNE - THE MAN
WITH THE HUGE STOMACH and I am a competitive eater.  Although I am
a tiny man (5 feet, 100 pounds alot of it is stomach) I eat large
amounts of food in short periods of time.  I have been featured on
German Television:  "TINY MAN EATING MACHINES".  Please put that
in all flyers.  I will eat 62 blueberry pies in 12 minutes.  I
have been sick only once.  It sounds funny, but a student had to
stand on my stomach and a stream of blueberry shot out after the
62nd pie.  I can laugh about it now but believe me we don't want
that to happen again especially in your outdoor area under the hot
sun in front of a lot of students calling for me to eat "one more
pie" and break my own record.  I will attempt 64 pies (2 more then
record) at Syracuse University.  Am I performing on the campus
lawn?  Please have the pies ALL blueberry.  i must be clear on
this as my last engagement the pies were mixed, some blueberry
some boysenberry and i was ill back at my room. (Student on
stomach, blueberry gush incident; will NOT pay for cleanup on
walls))  I need to be held in tight with a truss or rupture belt.

I will a arrive Morning of May 30.  Please tell me who I report
to.  Write me for measurements for rupture belt.  Thank you.

Sincerely,

F.D. Nancy
LORNE - THE MAN WITH THE HUGE STOMACH
```

April 20, 2009

Mr. F.D. Nancy
1413 ½ Kenneth Rd. #193
Glendale, CA 91201

Dear Mr. Nancy:

Thank you for your reminder of the Saturday, May 30th appearance at our University. However, I must admit that I have not been included in on the planning for this grand event. We have had several personnel changes here on campus and I fear the pertinent details may be with someone who no longer works at the University.

Would you be so kind as to inform me of the previous arrangements and expectations? Who did you work with in the past? I have checked the campus calendars and do not see an event of this magnitude on the schedule.

Additionally, I searched the Internet to discover more about your amazing talent, but was unable to find any details. Would you be so kind to provide me with more information and/or links to where I could find more?

If you so chose, you could communicate with me via email at dhall3@ju.edu.

Thank you,

Dr. Derek Hall
Vice President for University Relations
Jacksonville University

2800 University Boulevard North
Jacksonville, Florida 32211-3394
(904) 256-7000
Fax (904) 256-7012
1 (800) 225-2027
Web: http://www.ju.edu

F. D. NANCY
1413 1/2 Kenneth Rd. #193
Glendale, CA 91201

Book dept.
Mary Todd Lincoln House
578 W Main St, Lexington, KY 40504   Apr 5,2009

Dear Book department:

I am seeking a book, I don't know the name, but I was told you may
have it dealing with Mary Todd Lincoln. I think the name of the
book may be: THE CRAZINESS OF MARY TODD LINCOLN or something like
that. It deals with Mrs. Lincoln's madness. My neighbor, Inez,
claims to be a direct descendent of Mary Todd Lincoln. She is a
little batty, so who knows. She's always showing me a bunch of
clothes and stuff she said were worn by Mary Todd Lincoln. I have
to admit it is interesting to see the box of stuff she has,
dresses and shoes, and ribbons for the hair. Plus she has some
pictures and she's always babbling about one day she will donate
them to the proper place and then EVERYONE will know she really
was a relative of this fine first lady who was left all this
stuff, this box of cutlery, a wallet, etc. ANd I do have to admit
I have seen a few of the pictures of Mary Todd with the same
clothes on her. So who knows. Maybe my neighbor isn't so loopy
and out of it. That is why Id like that book. I think the name
of it is: THE LOONY-NESS OF MARY TODD LINCOLN.

My neighbor does resemble Mary Todd Lincoln, who I believe was a
very good First Lady that loved her beloved husband and was good
for our country. Maybe the name of the book is: THE LUNATIC
MARY TODD LINCOLN. I wish I could be more helpful. I know it
dealt with Mary Todd Lincoln supposedly being mad like my
neighbor. I'd love to buy a book from you. I think it may even
be out on audio (if there is such a book) that I believe Gary
Sinise reads the book. Thank you for trying to help me here.

Respectfully,

F.D. Nancy

Mary Todd Lincoln House, Lexington, Kentucky

This house in Lexington, KY was the girlhood home of
Mary Todd Lincoln, wife of President Abraham Lincoln.
She brought her husband and children to visit this
family home on several occasions.

Drawing by Miriam L. Woolfolk

4/9/09

Dr Mr/Ms Nancy (sorry I don't know which)
you are

The book you are looking for is called the
Madness of Mary Lincoln. We do
not carry it but you can probably
find it at most major bookstores in your
town. I would reccomend the new
book by Cathrine Clinton; Mrs.
Lincoln-a life.

I can not comment on your
neighbor's state of mind but I know
she is not a direct descendant of
Abraham + Mary as their last descendant

died in 1985. She may be a
descendant of the Todds as there
are many of us around (and we
are not all loony).

Good luck in your search.
Donna Holloway
Museum Store Manager

97

```
                              560 N. Moorpark Rd.  Apt #236
                              Thousand Oaks, CA 91360
```

CELEBRITY SHOE MUSEUM
Terry Hillgartner
3229 Alta Mere
Fort Worth, TX 76116

Dear Mr. Hillgartner,

I am writing to you because I understand you have a Celebrity Shoe
Museum. At last! I have been collecting celebrity shoes for
almost 80 years and now want to donate them to you. (some are
stinky) I know you will give them the best care.

I understand you are the only major shoe museum in the United
States. I have heard of one in Antwerp. But they display only
aviator shoes. Then there is one in Fiji that has only hospital
slippers. This is a much need celebrity shoe museum.

Please look at my shoes. And maybe my socks. I need this. I
have searched for shoes all over the world and have even taken
them off a sleeping celebrity. (after i darted him)

Let;s get this shoe thing going! I am more then ready. Frankly i
am sick of these shoes (some smell) I want to rid my home of
them. They are evil. One winked at me. They are nothing but
trouble. They have caused me grief. Would you like them? I
await your response.

Sincerely,

Ted L. Nancy

DALLAS
HOUSTON
FORT WORTH
SAN ANTONIO
DENVER

Mr. Ted L. Nancy
560 No. Moorpark Road Apt. #236
Thousand Oaks, CA 91360

Dear Mr. Nancy:

I am very interested in your 80 year quest of collecting
celebrity shoes. It seems the stories about how you
acquired these items may <u>upstage</u> the shoes themselves.

I have included some photos of my collection along with a
current list along with articles written about our famous
shoe musuem. Take note of the cases we use to enshrine each
individual shoe.

Please write me or call me collect at 817/731-4961. I would
love to talk about our collection and the possibility of
acquiring your collection to place in everlasting <u>memory</u> on
exhibit.

Very truly yours,

LARRY'S SHOES

Terry L. Hillgartner
Marketing Director

LARRY'S SHOES
CORPORATE HEADQUARTERS
!29 Alta Mere
Fort Worth, Texas 76116
817/731-4961
Fax 817/737-7258

1413 1/2 Kenneth Rd. #193
Glendale, CA 91201

MOIST TOWELETTES MUSEUM
Los Angeles, CA

Jul 13, 2009

Dear Moist Towelettes Museum.

I have a MOIST TOWELETTE from the Civil War. It was given to our
family and it's a wet thing in another thing that you rip. maybe
it's the oldest moist wet wipey thing around. Who knows about
these wipey things?

My neighbor, this Inez woman, who is a direct descendant of Mary
Todd Lincoln was left it with a bunch of her personal stuff and
she gave me this. She said Mary Todd used it to wipe her face
after she ate and to wipe her fingers after shaking hands with
soldiers. (and for lemon pie)

I give it to you if wou want. I always thought it should be in a
museum. Or if you want to see a picture? Do you have a museum?
Let me know.

Respect,

F.D. Nancy

SANTA CLARITA
CA 913 3 L
06 AUG 2009 PM

F. D. Nancy
1413½ Kenneth Rd.
#193
Glendale, CA 91201

1478

Dear F. D. Nancy,   7/31/9

    Thank-you for your
letter. I do have a museum,
most of the examples are
online. They are stored
safely. I'd love to include
your moist towelette in my
collection. The prospect
is very exciting because it
is the oldest! Please let
me know how to best get
it. Best regards, JB →
                        phone # on back

Kenosha Public Museums

MATTERS/EDUCATION

5500 First Aven

Kenosha, WI 5

SANDWICHES ARE GETTING bigger

D. NANCY
113 ½ KE
GLENDALE

"THEY LAUGHED AT ME WHEN I SAID
EVERYONE WILL EAT SUB SANDWICHES
IN THE FUTURE. EVEN THE GIRLS."

—THE EARL OF SANDWICH,
OCT. 1640

560 N. Moorpark Rd. Apt #236
Thousand Oaks, CA 91360

Administrative Services
CHINOOK WINDS CASINO
1777 NW 44th
Lincoln City, Oregon 91367

Dear Chinook Winds Casino,

I want to set up my ham sandwich booth in your mens room. I will
sell ham sandwiches in the restroom. People eat 'em up. Why not?
Can you think of a better place to sell ham sandwiches. (i can
not) Call me Ernesto when we first meet. It's for me.

I believe when a man finishes using the restroom he would want a
ham sandwich. If it were there. Why not have it there right for
him? Huh? It's an impulse buy that works 40% of the time.

This sign should be in the Mens Room mirror: <u>Yes! We Have The
Potty Melt.</u> Forget about Ernesto. Call me Miguel. I need this.

When a man comes out of the stall he can buy a ham sandwich from
my tiny booth. We have Virginia Ham. Try our sweetbread ham
combo. Ask for a number 3. Please DO NOT request pineapple on
your ham sandwich. I do not want to mess with this in the bath
room.

Please tell me how i set up my ham sandwich booth in your mens
room. I was told your casino was open to new opportunities in
your mens rooms.

Also, can you tell me what office i would contact to request
casino credit from Chinook Winds Casino? Thank you.

Sincerely,

Ted L. Nancy

CHINOOK WINDS CASINO

Ted L Nancy
560 N Moorpark Rd # 236
Thousand Oaks, CA 91360

Dear Mr. Nancy,

Your second request letter was forwarded to my attention. At this time all of our food purchases are made through local representatives in the food industry, such as American Food Services and SYSCO.

We thank you for your interest, but at this time we are not interested in putting any business in the restrooms. Our main function here at the facility is gaming. We also have 5 food outlets for our customers.

Again, thank you for considering us, but at this time we are fine. Good luck with your venture.

Sincerely,

Margo Norton
Purchasing Manager

CC: Roland Cunningham, CFO
     File

560 N. Moorpark Rd. Apt #236
Thousand Oaks, CA 91360

Jobs Department
City of Kirkland
CITY PERSONNEL
123 5th Ave
Kirkland, WA 98033-6121

Dear Jobs Department;

I am looking for a government position. I have been a judge of
cheese for 25 years in the private sector. While I like judging
cheeses it is time to look for more. I have judged gouda and
muenster and have a class B rating as a Brie magistrate. I WILL
NOT judge Monterey Jack. I have judged cheeses in 11 states.

I also have scrap cheese for sale. Would the government be
interested in this? This is 22,000 pounds of scrap cheddar.
(mild) Can be used for sandwiches. Goes good with ham
sandwiches.

Please write and let me know how I may get a government position
as a cheese judge. I will relocate to Kirkland which I understand
has a large cheese eating population.

Sincerely,

Ted L. Nancy

KIRKLAND

123 FIFTH AVENUE • KIRKLAND, WASHINGTON 98033-6189 • (206) 828-1100 • TTY (206) 828-2245

Ted L. Nancy
560 N. Moorpark Rd. #236
Thousand Oaks, CA   91360

Dear Mr. Nancy:

We received your letter and appreciate your interest in working for the City of Kirkland. Unfortunately, we don't have any openings in your area of interest.

The City of Kirkland has a strong employee wellness program. We have found with the increased interest and desire for a healthy lifestyle, the demand for low-fat cheese has overwhelmed the Kirkland market.

With the increase in development many local merchants are having problems with rodents. They might have an interest in your scrap cheese. I recommend contacting the Kirkland Chamber of Commerce.

"Gouda" luck in your job search.

Sincerely,

Annette Briggs
Human Resource Analyst

TED L. NANCY
1413 1/2 Kenneth Rd #193
Glendale, CA 91201
Tedlnancy1@gmail.com

Wits Language School
Wits University,
Private Bag X3,
PO Box 2050,
Johannesburg, South Africa   Apr 28, 2009
Email: wls@wits.ac.za

Dear Wits Language School

I saw your ad on the Internet while i was looking for pouch rash
cream. (I feed kangaroos.) I need to learn South African Sign
Language fast! I am starting a job in an Indian Casino in Primm
and there are Chinook supervisors there who i need to converse
with. They are mute & from South Africa. We will talk Mostly
about work but some non work conversing. Can you help?

Is this the same Chinook sign language I think it is?   A rapid
almost "yelling" language with some blurting?

My new co-worker went to you online and he learned much.
When does school start?   Send me info.

Sincerely,

Ted L. Nancy
Ted L. Nancy

South African Sign Language Courses

Juliet Mabjana
Tue, Jun 2, 2009 at 1:23 AM

TED L. NANCY <tedlnancy1@gmail.com>
Tue, Jun 2, 2009 at 9:31 AM

From: Juliet Mabjana <Juliet.Mabjana@wits.ac.za>
Date: Tue, 2 Jun 2009 10:23:34 +0200
Subject: South African Sign Language Courses
To: Tedlnancy1@gmail.com

Dear Nancy

Thank you for your enquiry about the SA Sign Language Courses. We offer part time SASL course and you have to attend classes in Johannesburg. We do not offer distance learning or online courses for SASL or any of our courses

SASL is a visual and manual language using hands, fingers, face and eyes. It does not have any sort of sounds. Since you are in the USA, it is advisable for you to learn American Sign Language because Deaf South Africans will understand the gist of what you are trying to say.

Regards,

Juliet Mabjana

African, Asian and European Languages
Wits Education Campus, Student Union Bldg

Short Courses Coordinator
St Andrews Road
011 717 3770
Parktown

```
                              F.D. NANCY
                              1413 1/2 Kenneth Rd. #193
                              Glendale, CA 91201
                              f.d.nancy@lycos.com




Reservations
Casa Delfino Hotel
9 Theofanus Street
73100 Chania
Crete, Greece
Email: info@casadelfino.com                    12 Apr 2009




Dear Casa Delfino Hotel:

I would like a reservation for 9 nights at your hotel.  You have
been highly recommended by the Pinecone Association Of Atlanta
where, I believe, many of our members have stayed.

I was hoping for a rate consideration and was told to contact the
hotel directly.  I am a traveler.

Info:  I will be arriving by sea shuttle on May 16, 2009 and
checking out May 23, 2009.  I may need a late check-out as I am
part of a Theater Group and will need to practice my two lines in
your lobby from 2 in the afternoon until 3:45.  I will say: "Is
Andy there?"  And "May I speak to Andy?" over and over again until
I am picked up for my performance.  Is that Okay?  I don't think I
will disturb others in your lobby as I will not YELL "Is Andy
There?"  I will just say it as in conversation.  Or perhaps you
can direct me to a room off the lobby where I may practice.  My
theater director Ediz Flacos asked me to practice around people as
I will miss the rehearsal because I am arriving late and the first
performance is that night.  So I will have to say "Is Andy there?'
And "May I speak to Andy?" over and over again for 2 hours.
However, I may say "Are you Andy?" (from time to time but not that
much)  That line MAY be in the play.  Will know that night.

Please confirm a suite for me from 16 May - 23 May.  Once again
you have been HIGHLY recommended from an individual in the Atlanta
area.  My sea shuttle number is 612-B17.  Thank you.  I am anxious
to eat at you Restaurant for your soup.  I await confirmation.

Sincerely,


F.D. Nancy
```

F.D. Nancy

From: Casa Delfino   **Sent:**   Sunday, 12 April, 2009
Message: Dear. Mr/Ms. F.D. Nancy,

We thank you for your e-mail and appreciate your interest in Casa Delfino Suites.
In reply to your room request we would like to inform you that we have availability
either in the Junior Suite, 1-Bedroom suite or 1-Bedroom apartment for the requested
period:

IN: 16th May 09
OUT: 23rd May 09
NIGHTS: 7

Daily rate for the 1-Bedroom apartment is 206,00 EURO, for the 1-Bedroom suite is
242,00 EURO and for the Junior Suite is 290,00 EURO.

We won't change you the rate on 17th May 09 like it's shown on our web page we will
keep it like it is.
If you would like to proceed on reservation, please provide us with your credit card
details until 14th April 09 at 12:00 local time.

Thank you and we look forward to your reply.

With kind regards,
Stella Tsismenaki
Reservations

Reservations
Casa Delfino Hotel
9 Theofanus Street
73100 Chania
Crete, Greece
Email: info@casadelfino.com   12 Apr 2009

Dear Casa Delfino hotel:

Thank you for your prompt reply. Your service is impeccable and
will be noted in my folder and shown to others.

Now down to my stay for 9 nights. What about the Play I am in and
the practicing of the Andy lines I must repeat in your lobby? Can
that be accommodated? Or can you suggest a room I may rent to do
this. (this will be for 2 hours. Re: "Is Andy there?") This is
an important production by the noted director of many musicals.
That is why we are in Crete.

I look forward to Greece and enjoying my stay at your highly
reommnded hotel.

Restfully,

F.D. Nancy

----- Original Message -----
From: CasaDelfino
To: info@casadelfino.com
Sent: Sunday, April 12, 2009 10:04 PM
Subject: Re: Casa Delfino:: Φόρμα Επικοινωνίας

9 THEOFANOUS str. 73100-CHANIA-CRETE-GREECE
TEL: +30-28210-87400/93098 FAX: +30-28210-96500
e-mail: *casadel@cha.forthnet.gr*
www.casadelfino.com

CASA DELFINO
S U I T E S

Dear Mr./Ms. Nancy,

First of all I would like to apoligize that I forgot to mention in my previous e-mail about your request in having a room or the lobby for practising your Andy line.
We can offer you with pleasure for two hours either the meeting room or the lobby as you like.

Please be so kind and inform us for which room category you would like us to book you in for the requested period (IN: 16th May 09   OUT: 23rd May 09   NIGHTS: 7).

Thank you and we look foward to hear from you soon.

With kind regards,
Stella Tsismenaki
Reservations

1413 1/2 Kenneth Rd. #193
Glendale, CA 91201
f.d.nancy@lycos.com

Reservations
Casa Delfino Hotel
9 Theofanus Street
73100 Chania
Crete, Greece
Email: info@casadelfino.com   14 Apr 2009

Dear Casa Del Fino Hotel.

Once again i must compliment you on your professionalism and i
will note it in my folder to show others. You are an outstanding
facility in the customer relations dept. I am impressed. and i
wish I could tell **EVEN MORE** peoples & others about your hotel in
Crete. Wonderful!

Now down to my stay for 9 nights May 16 May 23. I need to make
clear that my line has been changed to "Is Michael there?" and
"May I speak to Michael" (not Andy) Is that OK? Does that make
a difference? There may be a Michael there that would be insulted
but not an Andy. I am just checking to be civil. I'm really
going to have to rehearse now <u>3 hours</u> every day in your lobby as
this is sudden.

Please include a Mr. Roy Gum as my co-companion. How do we
proceed? I am looking forward to a relaxing stay (other then the
Michael lines I need to practice for 3/12 hours straight in your
lobby.) The service you give me is impeccable and Highly
regarded. I have already recommended your hotel to Michael, who
is the new lead in the play. He may take a room too. My sea
shuttle number has been changed to 612-D (not B) 17. I have been
upgraded to carrier class.

So what is next? I am anxious to finally get these reservations
completed. Do you have soup?

With Respects,

F.D. Nancy
F.D. Nancy
Jed (It's me)

Dialogue with Casa Delfino (latest appears in red)

From:	Casa Delfino	**Sent:**	Tuesday, 14 April, 2009

Message: If you want to go ahead with this booking, please click accept below to submit credit card details through the i-escape secure system, thank you.

Click to hide previous dialogue

From:	Casa Delfino	**Sent:**	Tuesday, 14 April, 2009

Message: Dear Ms./Mr. Nancy

Thank you for your kind words.

We would like to inform you that you can practise your lines in our lobby.

If you would like to proceed on reservation, please provide us with your credit card details until 15th April 09.

Thank you and we look forward to your reply.

Best regards,

Yiannis Chondrakis
Reservations

F. D. NANCY (MR)
1413 1/2 Kenneth Rd. #193
Glendale, CA 91201
f.d.nancy@lycos.com

Reservations
Casa Delfino Hotel
9 Theofanus Street
73100 Chania
Crete, Greece
Email: info@casadelfino.com   17 April 2009

Dear Casa Del Fino Hotel.

Again, my highest platinum, gold circle, cul de sac compliments to
you. (the highest in the real estate world.) Now. With regards
to my yelling out the name "Michael" in the lobby for 6 straight
hours... That is changed. I am now moving up to the part of
Michael. So I can't yell Michael out. The other Michael has
taken ill with Sars. I will now yell out "Is Tito there?" "May I
speak with Tito?" OK? Also can you recommend an actor to play
the role of Andy? He has come down with Swine Flu.

Once again: 12 nights May 16 May 26. Please include Roy Gum. We
made need a vinyl medical tent in the room . How do we proceed?
My sea shuttle number has been changed once again to BRAAAACK V-17
L-1.   Do you have bread? I await my conformation number.

Respectfully,

F.D. Nancy
(Michael)

NO FURTHER REPLY!

F. D. NANCY
1413 1/2 Kenneth Rd. #193
Glendale, CA 91201

Information
Civil War Museum
5400 First Avenue
Kenosha, WI 53140   5 Apr, 09

Dear Civil War Museum.

Someone told me you had a class in RUBBER STAMPING.

I will be in Kenosha all spring & summer as part of my rubber
stamp association group. This is a group that meets semi
quarterly and discusses rubber stamps and their history. Nothing
else. Two of our group members walked in front of a train.

How do I sign up?

We create many items such as cards and gifts with our rubber
stamps and am anxious for a few of us to attend your class. Our
life is rubber stamping. Nothing else. A past member jumped off
a roof.

Where do we sign up?

Thank you for writing me with information. All we talk about and
care about are rubber stamps. That's it. One group member lit
himself on fire in front of the rest of the group. Kenosha is a
beautiful city and is really the heart of Wisconsin. Not the
cheese.

Respectfully,

F.D. Nancy

F.D. Nancy

Kenosha Public Museum
5500 First Avenue
Kenosha, WI 53140
262.653.4140
www.kenoshapublicmuseum.org

Dinosaur Discovery Museum
5608 Tenth Avenue
Kenosha, WI 53140
262.653.4450
www.dinosaurdiscoverymuseum.org

Civil War Museum
5400 First Avenue
Kenosha, WI 53140
Opening in Spring 2008
www.thecivilwarmuseum.org

April 14, 2009

F. D. Nancy
1413 1/2 Kenneth Rd. #193
Glendale, CA 91201

Dear F. D.,

Thank you for your interest in the Kenosha Public Museums rubber stamping class. The class was scheduled to start this week but was canceled due to low registration. We will not be offering the rubber stamping class again until the fall. The only adult classes that we offer over the summer are basket making workshops.

If you'd like to check out some of our other classes and workshops they are all listed on our website at www.kenoshapublicmuseum.org.

If you have any questions about any of the Kenosha Public Museums and our educational programming, please feel free to contact me.

Sincerely,

I've enclosed the pages from the Spring program schedule that includes the classes & workshops.

```
                              F. D. NANCY
                              1413 1/2 Kenneth Rd. #193
                              Glendale, CA 91201




Information
Civil War Museum
5400 First Avenue
Kenosha, WI 53140                        18 May 2009



Dear Kenosha Civil War Museum.

Thank you for getting back to me and telling me the Rubber Stamp
Classes were canceled.  This depressed a group member and he
electrocuted himself in his bath tub.  He used Calgon bath
softener to relax then threw a fan in.  Went up like Cuban
Independence Day.

Now down to me.  I was told you had a class in WOODCARVING.  I
belong to a group & that is all we do.  Carve Wood.  I will be in
Kenosha in July as part of my wood carving group.  This is a group
that meets semi quarterly and discusses wood & carving.  Nothing
else.   We are dedicated.  Two of our depressed group members
jumped from a moving car on the Freeway.

How do we all sign up?

We create many items such as holders and gifts with our wood
carvings and am anxious for us to attend your class.  Our life is
wood. (and carving).  Nothing else.  A past member leaped from a
cliff.

Thank you for writing me with information.  All we talk about and
care about are wood carvings and metal feet.  That's it.  One
group member threw a rope over an exposed beam in his laundry
room, put it around his neck, and stepped off his hamper.  His leg
twitched.

Kenosha is a beautiful city and is really the heart of Wisconsin.
Not the sausage .  Can you book a private tour of the Civil War
Museum as i have heard?

Respectfully,
F. D. Nancy
F.D. Nancy (MR)
```

Thanks for your inquiry
but we do not have
cooking classes in
summer. For tour
information visit our
website www.thecivilwarmuseum.org

FD Nancy
1413 ½ Kenneth Rd
#193
Glendale CA
91201

UNITED STATES POSTAGE

PITNEY BOWES

POST CARD

02 1P $ 000.28⁰
03929121 MAY 29 2009
MAILED FROM ZIP CODE 53140

TED L. NANCY
560 No. Moorpark Rd. Apt #236
Thousand Oaks, CA 91360 USA

Disease Prevention Information
ARIZONA DEPT OF HEALTH SERVICES
2700 N 3rd St.
Phoenix, AZ 85004

Dear Arizona Disease Prevention Services:

I have a Disease question to ask you. I am leaving from Phoenix
by cattle on a trip:

I travel with 52 pictures of Popeye. I take ALL my Popeye
pictures with me when I go to a hotel. I will have 9 pictures of
Popeye on my dresser. I will put 14 pictures of Popeye near my
bed. I will hang SOME pictures of Popeye on the wall. (I use
Baboon Glue, the Popeye wall fastener). Will you wash my frog? I
even take 12 pictures of Popeye into the shower with me. Don't
worry they won't get wet. I hold them OUTSIDE of the shower while
the water is running on me. Who would want to get a picture of
Popeye wet? My dog smells?

I will bring my Bun Scruncher with me, is that ok? I need it! If
I am to have solid buttocks like my neighbors. I will work my
buttocks in my room. I work one buttock then I work the other.

My Disease question: Can I get a disease from cologne that I
bring back from a foreign visit? I believe this is scientific.
Cologne CAN cause disease. Thank you. I think the Disease Dept.
does a fantastic job. Please direct me to the proper place.

Respectfully,

Ted L. Nancy
Ted L. Nancy

Bureau of Public Health Statistics
2700 N Third Street; Suite #4075
Phoenix, Arizona 85004-1186
(602) 542-7331 Phone
(602) 364-0082 FAX
Internet E-mail: tflood@hs.state.az.us

JANE DEE HULL, GOVERNOR
JAMES L. SCHAMADAN, M.D., ACTING DIRECTOR

Ted L. Nancy
560 N Moorpark Rd
Apt # 236
Thousand Oaks, CA 91360

Dear Ted:

This letter is in response to an undated letter that was recently referred to my office.

There is no scientific reason to believe that foreign cologne would be more likely to cause disease than would domestic cologne.

Some persons are offended by the strong odor of cologne. If you are one of those persons, it would be best if you avoid cologne altogether. If you are still concerned about foreign cologne, then I would suggest that you bring your own when you travel.

Sincerely,

Medical Director

¯ Leadership for a Healthy Arizona ¯

BANNERS & SIGNS FOR LESS
23922 Crenshaw Blvd.
Torrance, CA 90505   Jul 28, 2009
info@bannerforless.com

Dear Sign Making Company,

I am opening a business soon and need a sign made.

I am opening next to a KOO KOO ROO Restaurant.

My business is called: I AM THE WALRUS. I need a sign that says
that.

Then I will put my sign next to the KOO KOO ROO restaurant.

So I will have one big sign that says:

I AM THE WALRUS KOO KOO ROO

Can you make? How much? When? I look forward to my sign.

With respect for others' businesses,

Ted L. Nancy

LARGE SIGN MADE

Banners & Signs 4 Less <general@bannerforless.com>
To: "TED L. NANCY" <tedlnancy1@gmail.com>

Tue, Jul 28, 2009 at 2:17

Hello,
What type of sign are you looking for? Do you have the sizes?
If you have the sign program for your property, we can review it.
--
Should you require additional information, please contact me directly.

Thank you,

Taylor Ton
Banners & Signs 4 Less
23922 Crenshaw Blvd.
Torrance, CA 90505
310.891.2399
310.891.2397 f
www.bannerforless.com

[Quoted text hidden]

MY FACE
(i combined
the 2)

"I DON'T LIKE FLAPPY THINGS."

—PHYLLIS MURPHY (A PERSON OF INTEREST),
WHEN I ASKED HER—WHY DON'T YOU GET A BIRD?

560 N. Moorpark Rd.
Suite #236
Thousand Oaks, CA 91360

Corporate Information
BLUE BIRD GRAPEFRUITS
10135 Mill Rd.
Peshashtin, WA 98847

Dear Bluebird Grapefruits:

I am looking to employ your grapefruit mascot, PULPY, for my ad
campaign. I have always enjoyed Pulpy and I think he would be a
fine addition to our new ads. I was wondering if you would give
me permission to use his likeness, name, and stomach size for our
newest bus bench advertising.

My advertising campaign is called "Granny Takes A Squirt". I will
show senior citizens taking a nice squirt of grapefruit juice in
their eye. Then with one eye shut tight like Popeye they will
say: "I eat grapefruit because Pulpy tells me too. Sometimes I
take it in the eye."

We could pick Pulpy up at the airport and drive him to the
Marriott where he can stay in the room with Frank.

We will do his laundry, then send it back to him.

Please advise on usage of Pulpy for our ads. If I have not
reached the correct division can you please tell me so? I was
told this is where I write to.

Thank you very much. I enjoy Bluebird grapefruits. They are good
in a high chair. I look forward to hearing from you soon.

Respectfully,

Ted L. Nancy

Blue Bird, Inc.
(509) 782-1216
Fax (509) 782-1818
P.O. Box 378
Peshastin, WA 98847

Ted L. Nancy
560 N. Moorpark Rd.
Suite #236
Thousand Oaks, CA 91360

Dear Mr. Nancy:

Blue Bird, Inc. received your letters addressed to our plants located at 1470 Walla Walla Ave., Wenatchee, WA 98801 and at 10135 Mill Road, Peshastin, WA 98847. Your letters referenced the use of a grapefruit mascot "PULPY" for your proposed advertising campaign. Unfortunately, you haven't reached the correct Blue Bird, Inc. and we have no idea as to how to help you reach the correct Blue Bird.

We do wish you success in your pursuit.

Sincerely,

Rhonda Stevens

Rhonda Stevens

1413 1/2 Kenneth Rd. #193
Glendale, CA 91201

May 19, 2009

Customer Help
TIME LIFE MUSIC
Po Box 4002011
Des Moines, Iowa 50340---2011

Dear Time Life Music:

I ordered Time Life Music's CRUNCHING NOISES OF THE 60'S. I have
not received it to date. I order a lot of music and this is the
first time it did notarrive.

I understand this comes with a bonus album of "SLAPPING SOUNDS OF
THE SEVENTIES" and I have not received that yet either. Where is
it? I have enjoyed many hours of your Time Life Music. Currently
I am listening to clapping and applauding all day long. I use it
for a play I am in where I shout out "Andy" in a Greece Hotel
lobby.

Please reply and tell me where my order is. Please send me a
catalog. Thank you.

Sincerely,

F.D. Nancy

F.D. Nancy (MR)

CUSTOMER CARE
7:00 am - 11:00 pm EST, 7 days a week

English	**Español**	**Canadian**
800-846-3543	800-882-0024	800-828-8565
TimeLife.com	TimeLifeEspanol.com	TimeLife.ca

PO Box 4002011
Des Moines, IA 50340-2011

May 29, 2009

Il.I.....Il.I.Ill.....Il..Il.l.Il...Il.l.I.I..Il.I.I

F D Nancy
#193
1413 1/2 Kenneth Rd
Glendale   CA 91201-1478

Account #: TML/TLU

Dear F D Nancy:

Thank you for contacting Time Life.

Thank you for your recent interest in our products. Unfortunately, we did not receive your order, and we are sorry to inform you that Crunching Noises is not one of our products.

We do not have a catalog available. If you have questions about a specific product, please contact our Customer Service Center.

If you have any questions, please contact our Customer Service Center.

A. Davis
Customer Care

109148093152002/MD00

F.D. NANCY (MR)
1413 1/2 Kenneth Rd. #193
Glendale, CA 91201

Information
Oakland Chamber of Commerce.
475 14th St #100
Oakland, CA 94612   Apr 25,2009

Dear Oakland Chamber Of Commerce,

I will be registering for the TINY MEN CONVENTION in your city of
June 1-9.

I hope I have reached the correct place. Can you please give me a
list of hotels that I can contact.

Hotels that cater to tiny men. We are not little people or dwarfs
or midgets. we are Tiny Men. That is fully proportioned men that
are 5 feet or less and no more then 100 pounds. (in wet clothing;
strict on this) I am a police officer in Ceylon so I have a
normal job even though I am a tiny man.

Also, I would like to purchase tickets to the performance of:
TINY BENNETT.   This is a tiny man that sings Tony Bennett.   He
is a petitio man (4'2") that looks EXACTLY like Tony Bennett and
sings pretty good like Tony. Tiny men from all over the world
will converge on your city. It will be exciting.

Please write me with hotel information so I can confirm my travel.
Thank you.

Sincerely,

F.D Nancy

F.D. Nancy

Please view attaching for our active
listing hotels.

I could not find anything on Tiny Bennett,
but I did attach a schedule for Tony.

475 14th Street, Oakland, CA 94612-1903
TEL: (510) 874-4800 FAX: (510) 839-8817
www.oaklandchamber.com

No results found for "tiny bennett"

tiny bennett

Search Results for "tony bennett" (9)

Other close matches: tiny kennedy, pinto bennett

Set Your Location	**United States Of America** (9)		
City or Zip Code	**Event**	**Location**	**Date ▾**
	Tony Bennett	**The Midland by AMC** Kansas City, MO	Sat, 05/02/09 08:00 PM
City			
Prior Lake, MN (2)	**Tony Bennett At N.O. Jazz & Heritage Festival 2nd Weekend**	**Small Venue Louisiana** NEW ORLEANS, LA	Multiple Dates and Times
Atlantic City, NJ (1)			
Cohasset, MA (1)			
Hyannis, MA (1)			
Kansas City, MO (1)	**Tony Bennett**	**Mystic Lake Casino Hotel** Prior Lake, MN	Sun, 05/10/09 07:00 PM
Lake Charles, LA (1)			
NEW ORLEANS, LA (1)			
Saratoga, CA (1)	**Tony Bennett Mother's Day Ticket Package * Sold Out!**	**Mystic Lake Casino Hotel** Prior Lake, MN	Sun, 05/10/09 - Sun, 05/10/09
Event			
Tony Bennett (9)			
New Orleans Jazz and Heritage Festival (1)	**Tony Bennett**	**L'AUBERGE DU LAC CASINO AND RESORT** Lake Charles, LA	Fri, 05/29/09 08:30 PM
Venue	**Tony Bennett**	**Caesars Atlantic City** Atlantic City, NJ	Fri, 07/10/09 10:00 PM
Mystic Lake Casino Hotel (2)			
Caesars Atlantic City (1)			
Cape Cod Melody Tent (1)			

Find Tickets (for 05/02/09)
Find Tickets (for N.O. Jazz & Heritage)
Find Tickets (for 05/10/09 07:00 PM)
Find Tickets (for Mother's Day)
Find Tickets (for 05/29/09)
More Info presale begins 04/30/09 10:00 AM

F.D. NANCY (MR)
1413 1/2 Kenneth Rd. #193
Glendale, CA 91201

Information
Oakland Chamber of Commerce.
475 14th St #100
Oakland, CA 94612   May 27, 2009

Dear Oakland Chamber Of Commerce.

Thank you so much for writing back and looking up Tiny Bennett for
me on Google. Hmm? I was sure he was performing at the TINY MAN
CONVENTION which will now take place on July 15-24 2009 instead of
June 1-9 which i was misinformed. In Oakland.

I am now told the singer will be SMALL MCCARTNEY which is a tiny
man singing Beatle songs. I would like to purchase tickets to his
performance. He is a petitio man (4'1") that looks EXACTLY like
Paul McCartney. Tiny men from all over the world will converge on
your city. It will be exciting. We have experienced BEATLE-MINIA
before. (People have passed out)

Can you tell me where Small McCartney will be performing? And can
you also send me info on car rental places?

The Oakland Chamber of Commerce truly cares. In this day and age
when no one cares. You care. It will be noted and shown to the
Winnebago Log Homes peoples.

Please write me with rental car information so I can confirm my
travel.

Thank you.

Sincerely,

F. D. Nancy

F.D. Nancy

METROPOLITAN CHAMBER OF COMMERCE
Serving the Business Community Since 1905

May 28, 2009

F.D. Nancy,

I can not find any information on the SMALL MCCARTNEY show. I've attached our Oakland Convention & Visitors Bureau and Oakland Coliseum's calendar, I hope the event you are interested is listed, if not, this is the best I can do. I've also attached a list of our members who may help you to rent a car while you are visiting. Please let us know if you have any questions.

Have a good day!

Oakland Metropolitan Chamber of Commerce

```
                              F.D. NANCY
                              1413 1/2 Kenneth Rd. #193
                              Glendale, CA 91201
```

Information
Jerusalem Chamber Of Commerce
10 Hillel Street,
P.O. Box 2083,
Jerusalem 91020, Israel   Apr 26, 2009

Dear Jerusalem Chamber of Commerce

I am seeking assistance. I am told that the TINY MAN CONVENTION
is to be held in Jerusalem June 1-9 2009. It may be held outside
the United States due to international interest in this event.
There will be 12,000 tiny men descending on your city. Tiny men
from all over the world (and one from Space) will converge on
Israel, eat your food, use your restrooms, date your women. We
are not dwarfs, or Midgets, or Fun Size People. We are Tiny Men.

What courtesies can i expect? What is the limit of Tiny Men in
your hotel rooms at any one time. We will hold a mixer in my
room. May have 54 miniature men in room lying on bed, sitting on
chairs, using up towels in bathroom. OK? Can you suggest a hotel
for me? Must be an approved TINY MAN HOTEL? certificate MUST be
displayed in lobby. Call me Ted L. Nancy when I first arrive and
am greeted at airport. I need that. I am a dentist in Ceylon. I
specialize in getting shredded beef out of teeth.

Your Chamber Of Commerce is highly praised and most well received
by those in the Chamber of Commerce business.

Thank you for your assistance. I await my reply on:

Tiny Man Convention June 1-9 2009
Tiny Man Hotel (approved)

Respectfully,

F. D. Nancy (signature)
F.D. Nancy
really Ted L. Nancy

לשכת המסחר ירושלים
JERUSALEM CHAMBER OF COMMERCE

רח' הלל 10, ת"ד 2083, ירושלים 91020 • טלפון 6254333/4/6 • פקסימיליה 6254335 (02)
10 Hillel St., P.O.B. 2083, Jerusalem 91020 Israel • Tel. 6254333/4/6 • Fax. (02) 6254335
E-mail: jerccom@inter.net.il • דואר אלקטרוני • http: www.jerccom.co.il :אתר אינטרנט

May 5, 2009

Mr. F.D. NANCY
1413 ½ Kenneth Rd. #193
Glendale, CA 91201
USA

Dear Sir:

We have just received your letter and after checking, we have not found
where the TINY MEN CONVENTION will be held in Jerusalem (June 1-9,
2009).

To our knowledge, there are not specific hotels for Tiny people.
But I advise you to see on the website of the Israeli Golden pages the
general list of Jerusalem hotels: **www.d.co.il.**

We wish you a pleasant stay in Jerusalem.

Yours sincerely,

Rahel Azoulay

135

F.D. NANCY (MR)
1413 1/2 Kenneth Rd. #193
Glendale, CA 91201

SWANSONS FROZEN DINNERS
Swanson Consumer Affairs
PO Box 91000
Allentown, PA 18109   May 26, 2009

Dear Swansons Dinners,

I am a long time eater of your Swansons Frozen TV Dinners.
Probably the finest combination of food I have ever eaten. I
stack 'em like medical trays in my freezer then pile them into me.
Someone at work told me you were coming out with:

SWANSONS FROZEN GASTRIC BYPASS DINNERS. It's all here. Country
Gravy, Buttered roll, pork chop, sugared yams, full 5 pound turkey
with all the trimmins'. And it's frozen. Thaw for 37 hours -
poke at it every now and then to see it is still rock solid ice -
and enjoy! Comes in Hearty Man size and XXL Hearty Man for the
300 pounder, 56 inch waister in your house. Free calm down wash
cloth included (to wipe your forehead after eating)

Is this for real? tell me it isn't. What's going on with this
country? Why would someone lie to me?

Anyway, can you please tell me if you still make Frozen Fried
Chicken Strips. I can NEVER find them. Please tell me you have
not discontinued this fabulous meal. I eat 6 a day. It's all i
eat. Now they are gone.

Thank you for answering my concerns. Swanson is a great food
company that many appreciate who can't cook so great.
I am a long time eater of your frozen food trays. My father
always says he is going to send me into space. And include a
stack of frozen Swanson dinners. (I do not believe him. he
drinks)

Respectfully,

F.D. Nancy

Pinnacle
FOODS GROUP LLC

June 4, 2009

Mr. F.D. Nancy
1413 1/2 Kenneth Road #193
Glendale, CA 91201

Dear Mr. Nancy:

Thank you for taking the time to contact us regarding Swanson® Dinners.
We genuinely appreciate your time and loyalty to our brand.

You may find the Swanson Frozen Fried Chicken Strips at the following
locations:

Food 4 Less
5420 W Sunset Blvd
Los Angeles CA 90027-5614
(323) 8718011

Food 4 Less
8035 Webb Ave
North Hollywood CA 91605-1505
(818) 2524855

At Pinnacle Foods Corporation, we are proud of the wide array of
products that we have to offer our consumers. Our brands are rich in
history and heritage, over 1,000 years combined, each one with a
different and interesting story. Breakfast, lunch, dinner or a snack,
Pinnacle Foods has your entire day covered! To learn more about our
brands and promotional activity, we invite you to visit us online at
www.pinnaclefoodscorp.com.

In appreciation of your loyalty, please accept the enclosed with our
compliments. If there is anything additional we can assist you with,
please do not hesitate to contact us again in the future.

Sincerely,

Consumer Insights Representative

001130419A

Did you know that

51351

5 51000 53101 3 (8101)0

FREE Swanson®
Swanson® Classics
Frozen Dinner
($1.50 Maximum Value)

1413 1/2 Kenneth Rd. #193
Glendale, CA 91201

Cruise Information
Cruise Deals Co.
11111 Carmel Commons Blvd.
Suite 210
Charlotte, NC 28226   6/10/9

Dear Cruise Deals.

I am interested in taking your cruise to Bermuda. This would be a
14 day cruise for myself and my companion Frito. All luxuries
please. Frito has a disability which i call your attention to:

Frito suffers from TOURETTES SIGN LANGUAGE. This is a form of
Tourettes Syndrome, which as you may know, is a medical disability
where one shouts out obscene words they cannot control.

Frito is a mute and cannot speak. So he makes obscene gestures at
strangers as they pass. Instead of spewing out a filthy stream of
vulgarities. Belive me, It can be quite troublesome to see an
innocent couple enjoying the splashing water and warm sun and
Frito approaches and gives them an obscene finger gesture or makes
the sign of the *&%# you. It can get worse as Frito currently has
17 obscene gestures and ticks he displays. I will be happy to
list all of them for you if you like. I keep a chart for travel
situations like this. But what can I do? Frito is my companion.

I will be arriving by raincage from Lodi. My Lodi # is K65D-*.
Can we make plans to go on a 14 day cruise, your finest
extravagances please? Frito shaves every 30 minutes. I look
forward to your reply with my request.

Sincerely,

F.D. Nancy
Frito likes limes.

Cruise Deals
11111 Carmel Commons Blvd. Ste. 210
Charlotte, NC 28226

June 16th, 2009

F.D. Nancy,

Thank you for allowing us to help you reserve your cruise vacation. I will work with the cruise line in any way possible to accommodate your needs for travel.

We can provide more information for your request but it will be best transmitted through email or telephone, I have listed my contact information below.

If you are unable to email or phone, I would need a few more bits of information to provide you with a cruise price.

-Dates you would be able to travel
-Departure city you prefer
-Unfortunately there are not any 14 day cruises offered to Bermuda, only 7 days with east coast departures. Is there another 14 day itinerary you would rather investigate, or would you like to quote the 7 day Bermuda itinerary?
-Cabin Category you prefer: inside, ocean view, balcony, suite

Thank you again for thinking of CruiseDeals.com for your vacation assistance. I look forward to working with you.

Best Regards,

Alara Shannon
CruiseDeals.com

Telephone: 800.668.6414 ext. 208
Email: ashannon@cruisedeals.com

1413 1/2 Kenneth Rd. #193
Glendale, CA 91201

Alara Shannon / Cruise Information
Cruise Deals Co.
11111 Carmel Commons Blvd.
Suite 210
Charlotte, NC 28226   8/3/2009

Dear Cruise Deal Company, MS Shannon.

I am sorry for the delay in replying. I have had my hands full
with Frito. I took him on a 12 day Safari Business Luncheon in
New Guinea and he had a relapse of his Tourettes Sign Language
problem. He made many disgusting signs at peoples AND animals.
(His Disease which i explained in prior letter: Frito suffers
from TOURETTES SIGN LANGUAGE. he is a mute and makes obscene
filthy vulgar gestures.) Finally he calmed down.

Now. Down to my relaxing cruise set up through you. As I believe
I mentioned in my first letter to you...I will be arriving by
raincage from Lodi. My Lodi # is K65D-**. They added an extra *.
We want to sail around Bermuda. 7 days as you suggested. Where
do we depart from?

The finest cabin. I think a breeze would be good for Frito. Let
him get some air on that face of his and get out of his cloud.

Please let me know all costs for this trip and fees for travel to
boat and back for 2. Luxury please.   We are ready for a relaxing
time.

Thank you,

F.D. Nancy

NO FURTHER REPLY!

140

1413 1/2 Kenneth Rd. #193
Glendale, CA 91201

Franchise Information
SWENSONS ICE CREAM
210 Shields Court
Markham, Ontario
Canada L3R 8V2   7/12/2009

Dear Swensons Ice Cream,

I am interested in investing money in SWENSONS ICE CREAM.
Swensons is the finest food co. out there and I have secured money
through a trampoline accident insurance payment and now want to
invest.

I have enjoyed SWANSONS FROZEN TV DINNERS for years. So what if
you're a letter off. It's just one letter. And now I am told you
will accept operators for your SWENSONS FROZEN TV ICE CREAM
DESSERTS. What a fantastic idea.

Please tell me how I can invest in a Swensons Franchise.

Thank you,

F.D. Nancy (signature)

F.D. Nancy

Dear F. D. Nancy,

Thank you for your interest in our company and concept.

The master franchise rights are presently available for Swensen's Ice Cream in California and we would be pleased to discuss this opportunity with you.

There are two formats to the Swensen's concept. The restaurant format and the ice cream parlour format.

We invite you to visit our website at www.swensensicecream.com to learn more about America's favorite ice cream that is "Good as Father Used to Make".

We are now focused on our global expansion plan and are seeking qualified franchise partners to grow with us.

The next step in our new business development process will be to have you complete the attached Franchise Application Form and return it to us by **fax to (905) 479–5235**.

If you have any further questions, please contact me.

Sincerely,

dave craig
business development

t: 905.479.8762 x 241
f: 905.479.5235
e: dcraig@swensensicecream.com

210 shields court : markham : ontario
L3R 8V2 : canada

www.swensensicecream.com

dave craig
director, business development

t: 905.479.8762 x 241
f: 905.479.5235
e: dcraig@yogenfruz.com

210 shields court : markham : on
L3R 8V2 : canada

www.yogenfruz.com

Subsidiary of International Franchise Corp.

F.D. NANCY (MR)
1413 1/2 Kenneth Road
#193
Glendale, CA 91201
U.S.A.

9120131478 C008

1413 1/2 Kenneth Rd. #193
Glendale, CA 91201

Mr. Dave Craig.
SWENSONS ICE CREAM
210 Shields Court
Markham, Ontario   August 10, 2009
Canada L3R 8V2

Dear Mr. Dave Craig.

I once knew 2 people. One was a David & the other a Craig. Funny
world. Now. Thank you for writing me back. I have always
admired both Swansons AND Swensons.

My question: Are you Swensons or Swansons? Or Yogen Fruz as your
envelope and card say. I looked up Yogen Fruz . It seems to be
some sort of squishy freezee dessert squashee. What is it? I
wanted FROZEN BY-PASS GASTRIC TV DINNERS. With all the trimmins'.
Turkey, mashed potatoes, cornbread, & ice cream.

But this Yorgen stuff looks very good. What is Fruz? I can
figure out was Yogen is.

So now i am really interested.   When do we start? How do we
begin? What is happening?

Sincerely,

F.D. Nancy (signature)
F.D. Nancy

1413 1/2 Kenneth Rd. #193
Glendale, CA 91201

BEN GAY   Jul 23, 2009
JOHNSON & JOHNSON
P.O. Box 726
Langhorne, PA 19047-0726

Dear Ben Gay People:

I am a long time user of Ben Gay. I am told you are changing your
name to BEN GOO. why?

I have used Ben Gay to satisfaction for years. It is the finest
goo out there but to change your name....

Benjamin Gay, I can see. Please! Don't.

I await my reply with the correct information.

Sincerely,

F. D. Nancy

INFORMATION
CENTER
199 Grandview Road
Skillman, NJ
08558-9418

July 23, 2009

F. D. Nancy
1413 1/2 W Kenneth Rd
193
Glendale, CA 91201-1478

Dear F. D.:

Thank you for contacting Johnson & Johnson Consumer Companies, Inc., makers of Original Strength BENGAY®
Pain Relieving Cream. It is always important to hear from our consumers, and we appreciate the time you have
taken to contact us.

We would like to answer your question in this letter; however in this case, we would be better able to help you over
the phone.

Please call the Information Center toll free at 1-800-223-0182 Monday through Friday between the hours of 8 AM
and 8 PM.

Be sure to mention the reference number below when you call.

We appreciate the opportunity to speak with you and apologize for any inconvenience.

Sincerely,

Robert D.
Consumer Care Center

008310007A

```
                              1413 1/2 Kenneth Rd. #193
                              Glendale, CA 91201




Mr. Robert D.
BEN GAY
c/o JOHNSON & JOHNSON
199 Grandview Rd
Skillman, NJ  08558-9418          Aug 3, 2009




Dear Ben Gay and Mr. Robert D,

Thank you for answering my letter:  That Ben Gay is changing its
name to BEN GOO.  You asked me to call you in answering my letter?
Why?  why do you need to help me over the phone? Huh?  Just
answer me.  Are you changing your name from BEN GAY to BEN GOO?
(as i have heard)  I am mentioning the reference number to you.
008310007A which is coincidentally numbers i have used before in
various combinations.

It's no big deal.  I was just at my desk when someone casually
said "I heard Ben Gay is changing its name to Ben Goo."  That's
all, nothing more.  It is goo isn't it?  I also heard you may
change it to:  Ben Gooey.  Which sounds to me like the former
Israeli Prime Minster.

Thank you for caring about us ointment users.  Ben Gay is the
finest ointment out there.




Signed,
Ben Gay Curious
(F.D. Nancy)
```

August 11, 2009

F. D. Nancy
1413 1/2 W Kenneth Rd
193
Glendale, CA 91201-1478

Dear F. D.:

Thank you for contacting Johnson & Johnson Consumer Companies, Inc., makers of Original Strength BENGAY®
Pain Relieving Cream. It is always important to hear from our consumers, and we appreciate the time you have
taken to contact us.

We have no plans to change the name of our BENGAY® Pain Relieving Cream.

Again, thank you for your interest in our company. Should you have any comments or questions in the future,
please contact us via our website or by calling our toll-free number, 1-800-223-0182. Our specialists are available
Monday through Friday between 8 AM and 8 PM EST and will be happy to assist you.

Sincerely,

Robert D.
Consumer Care Center

008310007B

BEN GOO MARTIAL ARTS

1413 1/2 Kenneth Rd #193
Glendale, CA 91201

Administration
FEDERAL CORRECTIONAL INSTITUTION
YAZOO CITY
2225 Haley Barbour Parkway
Yzzoo City, MS 39194   Nov 26, 2009

Dear Yazoo City Prison:

I own a Mixed Martial Arts School where we teach the ancient
fighting style of BEN GOO, a martial arts involving Judo, Karate,
& Pinching.

As part of my "Afternoon Stress Program" i would like to come to
your prison and put on a Ben Goo demonstration for your prisoners
& guards. There will be kicking and grunting and Kung Foo, and
some arm waving. We are in line with current MMA fighting rules.

Then i will give everyone in your prison a Swansons TV Dinner for
your prisoners to enjoy. Includes turkey, cranberries, stuffing,
cornbread, hot vegetable .

I have done this before and was only robbed once. We bring 22
fighting men for full Ben Goo martial arts demonstration which
includes Jiu-Jitsu, kickboxing, grabbing. When can we schedule
this and my Swansons gift? We are NOT Ben Gooey. That is not us.
It is my privilege to entertain your staff and prisoners.

The School is under the direction of Roy Tonsil. A 5th degree
Sansa Belt. He was a referee for 4 years. Then he was not.

Thank you,

F.D. Nancy

U. S. Department of Justice
Federal Bureau of Prisons
Federal Correctional Complex

P.O. Box 5666
Yazoo City, Mississippi 39194

December 9, 2009

F.D. Nancy
1413 ½ Kenneth Road #193
Glendale, California 91201

Dear Mr. Nancy:

This is in response to your correspondence dated November 26, 2009, concerning your offer for members of your martial arts school to provide a demonstration for the inmates and staff at the Federal Correctional Complex, Yazoo City, Mississippi,

For security reasons, Federal Bureau of Prisons inmates are prohibited from demonstrating, practicing or using martial arts, boxing, wrestling or other forms of physical encounter. For this reason, I believe that a martial arts demonstration would send an inappropriate message to the inmate population. Therefore, I must decline your offer.

I trust you will understand my position on this matter.

Sincerely,

Bruce Pearson
Warden

BENJAMIN GOOEY KABUKI

1413 1/2 Kenneth Rd #193
Glendale, CA 91201

Warden Bruce Pearson
FEDERAL CORRECTIONAL INSTITUTION
YAZOO CITY
2225 HALEY BARBOUR PARKWAY
YAZOO CITY, MS 39194   Jan 2, 2010

Dear Warden Pearson, Yazoo City Prison:

Thank you for your reply to my letter of a free show for your
prisoners and guards. And yes, I totally understand your
position of not allowing it. I am respectful.

I was wondring...as part of my "GIVE BACK AND FEEL GOOD PROGRAM"
would your prison be interested in my theater presentation
BENJAMIN GOOEY KABUKI ?

This is a kabuki-mime demonstration including walking against the
wind, stuck in a box, opening a window, getting in your face,
pinching. It is a softer show, one that has dancing waters,
windchimes, incense, and sprinkly rain. Kabukis and mimes dancing
around for all is relaxing. I would put it on in your prison yard
for all your prisoners and guards. We travel with 47 kabukis and
mimes. (when available; have skeleton mime crew)

Everyone then gets a Chinese dinner takeout incl. shrimps, paper
chicken, beef broccoli, tangy scallops. Please no substations.
(when available; do have snacks if not available) Then as part of
my DO GOOD FOR OTHERS PROGRAM i gift your entire prison with
shoes. These are the popular Waitermelons. I just need
everybody's shoe size. (currently out of 8, 9, 9 1/2, & 10. I do
have 11 extra narrow; all shoes when available)

I would be honored to put on this free show for Yazoo Prison, a
city of which I hold the fondest memories of..

Respectfully,

Ted L. Nancy

Ted L. Nancy

U. S. Department of Justice
Federal Bureau of Prisons
Federal Correctional Complex

P.O. Box 5666
Yazoo City, Mississippi 39194

December 9, 2009

Ted L. Nancy
1413 ½ Kenneth Road #193
Glendale, California 91201

Dear Mr. Nancy:

This is in response to your correspondence dated January 2, 2010, concerning your offer for members of your martial arts school to provide a demonstration for the inmates and staff at the Federal Correctional Complex, Yazoo City, Mississippi. You indicate that the presentation would be softer than your original offer to provide a fighting demonstration.

As mentioned previously, for security reasons, Federal Bureau of Prisons inmates are prohibited from demonstrating, practicing or using martial arts, boxing, wrestling or other forms of physical encounter. While I appreciate your offer, I continue to believe that a demonstration by individuals affiliated with a martial arts school would send an inappropriate message to the inmate population. Therefore, I must again decline your offer.

I trust you will understand my position on this matter.

Sincerely,

Bruce Pearson
Warden

GOOEY BEN OINTMENT

1413 1/2 Kenneth Rd #193
Glendale, CA 91201

Warden Bruce Pearson
FEDERAL CORRECTIONAL INSTITUTION
YAZOO CITY
2225 HALEY BARBOUR PARKWAY
YAZOO CITY, MS 39194   Jan 23, 2010

Dear Warden Pearson, Yazoo City Prison:

Thank you once again for answering me. For the record I am a long
time Yazoo descendent. My father was a Yazoo and his father was a
Yazoo. We are all Yazoos. That is why I want to reach out to
Yazoo Prison and give back. (for my program)

I manufacture an ointment - GOOEY BEN - which is a deep
penetrating pain cream. "Fast relief from minor arthritis,
backache, muscle & joint pain." Compares to BEN GAY.
"Temporarily relieves the minor aches and pains of muscles and
joints associated with simple backache, arthritis, & strains."

Stop use and ask a doctor if condition worsens or symptoms persist
for more than 7 days or excessive skin irritation occurs.

I would like to come to Yazoo and give everyone a tube of Gooey
Ben. (If available) Guards, prisoners. I am a professional!
How's that? Then I am giving back. (for my program) No
fighting, wrestling, pinching. Just nice soothing ointment. For
you. And all the people of Yazoo. (if I have) Gooey Ben is deep
penetrating pain relief. "Non-staining, goes on smoothly. With
three pain relieving ingredients - more then any other ointment.
Strongest GOOEY BEN® ever."

When using this product avoid contact with eyes or mucous
membranes, do not bandage tightly.

What do you think? Everyone feels better with ointment on them.
Let me know.

Respectfully,

Ted L. Nancy

Ted L. Nancy

U. S. Department of Justice
Federal Bureau of Prisons
Federal Correctional Complex

P.O. Box 5666
Yazoo City, Mississippi 39194

February 11, 2010

Ted L. Nancy
1413 ½ Kenneth Road #193
Glendale, California 91201

Dear Mr. Nancy:

This is in response to your correspondence dated January 23, 2010, concerning your request to visit the Federal Correctional Complex, Yazoo City, Mississippi, to promote an ointment that you manufacture.

It is not our practice to permit businesses to enter our facility to promote products. While I appreciate your offer, I must humbly decline.

I trust you will understand my position on this matter.

Sincerely,

Bruce Pearson
Warden

HERSHEY'S

The Hershey Company
100 Crystal A Drive
P.O. Box 810
Hershey, PA 17033-0810

86 JMECW31 91201

GLENDALE CA 91201-1478

is help on
the way?

PRESORTED
FIRST CLASS

049J62048601
$00.357
12/05/2009
Mailed From 18706
US POSTAGE

neopost

```
                                    TED L. NANCY
                                    560 N Moorpoark Rd #236
                                    Thousand Oaks, CA 91360
```

MR. THOMAS KLESTIL
Prasidententschaftskanzlei
Hofburg, 1014 Vienna, Austria

Dear Mr. President Klestil,

As President of Austria I am sure you get many many good letters.
(That's 2 manys)   Yes this is a good letter on my desire for
Austria and the fantastic job you are doing as it's leader.
BETRACHTILCH!

The people of Austria are wonderful. One helped me with a tar-y
heel i had stuck in a hot sidewalk. He pulled me free.

I have enjoyed my stay in Austria so much (where I stuffed my face
with gimelkronk) that I now want to become Austrian. I will
inject myself with Austrian spoongle and become a citizen. one of
you. How's that for dedication? Will you pet my dog? I want to
turn myself Austrian. I will take the needed injections and
ointments and live and work as an Austrian. BIMMELFARB!

I do this to salute you, and the gentleman that helped me change a
tire when i blew one out and veered off in a crowd of people at an
Austrian busstop and got my shoe stuck in the sidewalk.

Thank you for my reply. Please thank everyone for me.

Respectfully,

Ted L. Nancy
Future Austrianer
```
```

The Consul General of Austria

No. 3924/96

Dear Mrs. Ted,

I refer to your kind letter to the Austrian Federal President Thomas Klestil, which I have been asked to reply to, because President Klestil is in the hospital right now.

I thank you very much for your friendly words about the Austrian people. I am gratified to read that you enjoyed your stay in Austria as well as Austria's hospitality and the helpfulness of the Austrian people.

Sincerely yours,

Mag. Werner Brandstetter

Mrs. Nancy L. TED

560 No. Moorpark Rd. # 236
Thousand Oaks, CA. 91360

1413 1/2 Kenneth Rd. #193
Glendale, CA 91201
Ted1nancy1@gmail.com

Invention Information
Davison Inventions
RIDC Park
595 Alpha Dr.
Pittsburgh, PA 15238-2911   Jul 27, 2009

Dear Davison Inventions:

I need you to look at my invention: THE TELEPHONE. This is a
device that sits on a table, a wall, or held in your hand that has
numbers on it. It works like this: You dial a number. It rings
at another TELEPHONE. They say "hello" or "Yo" or some greeting
to let you know they answered. You then speak clearly into the
receiver and say: "Is Andy There?"

Please send me information on how I may register this with you. I
look forward to my paperwork.

Sincerely,

Ted L. Nancy
Ted L. Nancy

RE: The idea is finally getting the start it needs

Brad Mocharko   Jul 28 (5 days ago)

tedInancy1@gmail.com
Tue, Jul 28, 2009 at 12:56
PM
RE: The idea is finally getting
the start it needs
davison.com
davison.com

Hello TED,

I'd like to commend you for taking control of your idea concept. You're one step closer to having the personal satisfaction of inventing & pursuing an idea.

Per our conversation today, you agreed:

1. To return the signed documents & retainer payment for Pre-Development by no later than (date unavailable) and;
2. To phone me with the tracking numbers for your package (if applicable).

As I mentioned, TED, there are always reasons why clients may put off taking action, but they realized that if they don't put their foot down and take charge of their ideas, they may spend years wondering what could have been.

I can see from our call today that you are committed to seeing your idea come to life!

When we speak again, we will establish a schedule for future discussion about your idea.

TED, this is the beginning stages of our process of getting the idea ready to go to a corporation to see if they would be interested in acquiring it.

I'm looking forward to experiencing this with you!

Creatively Yours,
Brad Mocharko
Director of New Products
DAVISON | RIDC Park . 595 Alpha Drive | Pittsburgh, PA 15238
866-Davison ext. 50358 | Fax: 412-967-0794

1413 1/2 Kenneth Rd. #193
Glendale, CA 91201
Ted1nancy1@gmail.com

Brad Mocharko
Davison Inventions
RIDC Park
595 Alpha Dr.
Pittsburgh, PA 15238-2911   Aug 2, 2009
mocharko.brad@davison.com

Dear Mr. Brad Mocharko:

I once knew a Mr. Brad in the fastening business is that you? Now down to us. When did we have a conversation? Huh? I checked my conversation log and we are not on there. Yes! I am committed to seeing my idea come to life.

We need to establish a schedule for future discussions. However I am having trouble with my TELEPHONE. It does not work. No busy signal. That's why we did not talk today.

Now let's talk inventions! I need you to look at my invention: THE TELEVISION. This is a box that sits on a table with a screen in it. It works like this: You stare at it and tiny people move around. Some of them walk, some talk, others race around in cars. Some say: "Is Andy There?"

Please send me information on how I may register this with you. I look forward to my paperwork.

With Utter Respect For Inventions,

Ted L. Nancy

Ted L. Nancy

560 N. Moorpark Rd.   #236
Thousand Oaks, CA 91360

Reservations
ATLANTA HILTON HOTEL
255 Courtland St., N.E.
Atlanta, GA   30303

Dear Sir or Madam:

I am in the semi process of making partial reservations at your
hotel in Atlanta. (week of Sep 27) For me there is no finer
hotel than the Hilton. But that's for me. I have a request:

<u>My request:</u> I will be carried into your hotel on my special
chair. I will have many mens lift me into your lobby and around
your hotel on my throne like chair that I like to be carried on
throughout my stay. These mens have muscles.

<u>Places I will be carried:</u> Your lobby, through your coffee shop,
by the pool, into my room. My mens will be dressed as any mens
dress when carrying a guest in a kingly chair. (for the record it
is a swimming pool chaise lounge with vinyl straps but made to
look like a throne. I have had wet swim wear on it before)

Naturally i will remove all doors to my room, most windows, and
the shower nozzle. Can you help with my reservation? l will
arrive by Crab Boat shortly.

Respect for the Hilton,

Ted L. Nancy

Atlanta
Hilton
and Towers

Mr. Ted L. Nancy
560 N. Moorpark Road, # 236
Thousand Oaks, California 91360

Dear Mr. Nancy:

I received your recent letter requesting approval to bring your lounging chair during a future stay with us at the Atlanta Hilton & Towers.

It is our intention to absolutely ensure that our guests have a comfortable stay and that all the facilities provided are adequate to your needs. While there are no restrictions, per se, to you bringing your personal chair, we cannot allow the removal of any fixtures.

Mr. Nancy, I assure you that our accommodations are very comfortable and we can maximize your comfort in one of our newly renovated rooms. Please let me know if I can be of assistance to you in making your upcoming reservations. I can be reached on (404) 222-2952.

Sincerely,

Vijay Bahl
Assistant Director of Front Office Operations

VB/sdp

Courtland and Harris Streets Northeast, Atlanta, Georgia 30303   Telephone 404-659-2000
Reservations 1-800-HILTONS

1413 1/2 Kenneth Rd. #193
Glendale, CA 91201

Business Licenses
City Of Glendale
613 East Broadway, Room 110
Glendale, California 91206-4393   Apr 18, 2009

Dear City Of Glendale Business License dept:

I am seeking some help, please. Can you tell me what happened to
my application for my business license? I sent in paperwork and
filing fees for my comedy club: THE JOKESTRAP.

And it has been some time since I heard from you. Perhaps i was
sent to the wrong office. But i mailed many papers to your city
offices.

The JOKESTRAP is a comedy club, 17 tables, in a mini mall that I
am renting space from. All guffaw signs have been made, all t-
shirts paid for, (including 4XL which is costly), all comedy club
food incl. nachos and fried cheese yums on order. (we may have
burnt almond cheese straws)

So can you PLEASE tell me how I get my license and what happened
to my application? I have copies of everything if you need. Let
me know.

I admire your city. I am ready to open. I hire locally and use
local cheese.

Respectfully,

F.D. Nancy
F.D. Nancy

April 22, 2009

F.D. Nancy (MR)
1413 ½ Kenneth Rd. # 193
Glendale, CA 91201

RE: The Jokestrap- Comedy Club

Dear Applicant:

This is in response to your letter requesting status of your application for a business license in the City of Glendale. Depending on the location and nature of your business, you are required to apply for a Zoning Use Certificate.

The Building Department has not received such an application or any paperwork regarding your business. Enclosed you will find a packet indicating what the application process is as well as an application for you to complete and return to our office.

Please make sure to mail your correspondence to:

Building and Safety
633 E. Broadway, Room # 101
Glendale, CA 91206

If you have any questions or concerns regarding this matter, you may contact our Department at (818) 548-3200.

Yours truly,

Celeste Luna, OSS

Room 100   Inspections (818) 548-4836 FAX (818) 548-4362
Room 101 Applications, Plan Check & Permits (818) 548-3200 FAX (818) 548-3215

WE RECYCLE

164

F.D. NANCY (MR)
1413 1/2 Kenneth Rd. #193
Glendale, CA 91201

Business Licenses
CITY OF DOWNEY
11111 Brookshire Avenue
Downey, CA 90241   Nov 27, 2009

Dear City Of Downey Business License dept:

Can you please help me. It is been some time since I sent in my
application & fee for my comedy club: JOKE ITCH. Can you tell
me what happened to my application for my business license? Is it
still being processed?

JOKE ITCH is a comedy club, 22 tables, in an industrial area. All
giggle signs have been made, all Snuggies paid for, (including
6XL), all comedy club food including fried pretzels, cheese yanks,
and slaw daddies are on order. (we may have cheese cups;
definitely cheese bags)

So can you PLEASE tell me how I get my license and what happened
to my application? I have copies of everything if you need. (May
be under earlier name of JOKE CHAFE)

I admire your city. I am fully ready to open. I hire locally and
use local cheese.

Respectfully,

F. D. Nancy

F.D. Nancy (MR)

City of Downey

FUTURE UNLIMITED

December 10, 2009

F.D. Nancy (MR)
1413 ½ Kenneth Road #193
Glendale, CA 91201

Subject: Business license for Joke Itch or Joke Chafe

Dear Mr. Nancy

Thank you for your letter, dated November 27, 2009, regarding your pending application for a business license with the City of Downey. Unfortunately, the City of Downey has no existing records for an application of a business license for the comedy club JOKE ITCH or JOKE CHAFE. Please provide an address so the city can research the matter further.

Notwithstanding the submittal of a business license, the City of Downey Municipal Code requires approval of a Conditional Use Permit, prior to commencing business with live entertainment (including comedy clubs). The Conditional Use Permit is a discretionary action, which requires a public hearing before the City's Planning Commission. Furthermore live entertainment may not be permitted within all zones of the city.

If you have any questions regarding this matter, please feel free to call me at (562) 904-7154 or email me at srodriguez@downeyca.org.

Sincerely,

Sebastian Rodriguez
Planning Intern

F.D. NANCY (MR)
1413 1/2 Kenneth Rd. #193
Glendale, CA 91201

Mr. Sebastian Rodriguez, Planning Intern
Business Licenses
CITY OF DOWNEY
11111 Brookshire Avenue
Downey, CA 90241   Dec 18, 2009

Dear Mr. Sebastian Rodriguez, City Of Downey:

Thank you for writing me back on my business license. Downey is a
city that should be proud of the care its employees take to help
others.

I believe my application for my Comedy Club was filed under the
name: JOKE OINTMENT. Can you please check for me on this?

JOKE OINTMENT is a comedy club, 41 tables in a medical area. All
har har signs have been made, all paper cups paid for, all comedy
club food is on order including fried waffles, cheese tugs, and
dippin' sauce. (we may have cheese cups; definitely cheese shout
outs)

We have already hired our Headlining act, booked and paid for:
Tickles The Diseased Clown. Come in for a free Tater Squinch. We
leave the eyes on.

So can you PLEASE tell me how I can finally get my license and
what happened to my application so i can open in this medical area
for a successful business in your city? I have copies of
everything if you need. (May be under earlier name of JOKE SALVE)

Once again, I sincerely appreciate your help in this matter.

Respectfully,

F.D. Nancy

F.D. Nancy

City of Downey

February 17, 2009

F.D. Nancy (MR)
1413 ½ Kenneth Road #193
Glendale, CA 91201

Subject: Business license for Joke Ointment

Dear Mr. Nancy

Thank you for your letter, dated December 18, 2009, regarding your pending application for a business license with the City of Downey. Unfortunately, the City of Downey has no existing records for an application of a business license for the comedy club JOKE OINTMENT. At this moment we request for you to please come to the planning counter at city hall to resolve this matter.

Notwithstanding the submittal of a business license, the City of Downey Municipal Code requires approval of a Conditional Use Permit, prior to commencing business with live entertainment (including comedy clubs). The Conditional Use Permit is a discretionary action, which requires a public hearing before the City's Planning Commission. Furthermore live entertainment may not be permitted within all zones of the city.

If you have any questions regarding this matter, please feel free to call me at (562) 904-7154 or email me at srodriguez@downeyca.org.

Sincerely,

Sebastian Rodriguez
Planning Intern

```
                                    1413 1/2 Kenneth Rd. #193
                                    Glendale, CA 91201




Business Licenses
CITY OF NORWALK
12700 Norwalk Blvd
Norwalk, CA 90650                    Dec 7, 2009




Dear City Of Norwalk,

Can you tell me what happened to my application for my business
license?  I own a comedy club called:  JESTICLES.

I had sent in the paperwork and fees and have not received
anything to date.  JESTICLES is a 150 seat comedy club in your
city that I am opening.  We will have food.  (taters)

I had filled out all the papers and stamped them and my check has
been cashed.  Papers were filled out by our manager Marteen Lim.
Corky Chocolo is our opening headliner.  Followed by Bill Peeps.
They have been paid.  My FLYER is printed up and distributed.

I was told to write you with this information when I called to
track this down.

Thank you for your help.


Respectfully,
```

F.D. Nancy (signature)

```
F.D. Nancy
```

City Of Norwalk
12700 Norwalk Blvd.
Norwalk, CA 90650
(562) 929-5713
Fax # (562) 929-5056

December 16, 2009

Jesticles
C/O F. D. Nancy
1413 ½ Kenneth Rd #193
Glendale, CA 91201

Dear Business Owner:

The City of Norwalk requires all organizations operating within the City to have a business license. However I don't believe that you filed a business license application with the City of Norwalk. I have checked our files and have found no record of an application being filed or a check being cashed for a comedy club named Jesticles, of course it would have helped had you provide the address / location of this comedy club. We only issue business licenses to businesses that are either located or operating in the City. Perhaps you filed your application with the Los Angeles County Recorder's Office here in Norwalk; it is located at 12400 E. Imperial Hwy., Norwalk, CA 90650.

If you have any questions, please feel free to call the Business License Department at 562-929-5713.

Sincerely,

Paul Weldon
Business License/Revenue Section
City of Norwalk

12700 NORWALK BOULEVARD
P.O. BOX 1030
NORWALK, CA 90651-1030

ADDRESS CORRECTION REQUESTED

BUSINESS LICENSE

Jesticles
C/O F. D. Nancy
1413 ½ Kenneth Rd #193
Glendale, CA 91201

9120181421 C008

1413 1/2 Kenneth Rd. #193
Glendale, CA 91201

Liquor Licenses
CITY OF PALMDALE
38300 Sierra Highway
Palmdale, CA 93550   January 3, 2010

Dear City Of Palmdale.

I am looking to see what happened to my liquor license application
for my comedy club: SOMETHING SMELLS FUNNY

I sent in the paperwork and $92.00. I have not heard anything.
SOMETHING SMELLS FUNNY is a 72 table comedy club in your city that
is opening very soon. We will have liquor, beer, wine, fizzies,
chugalugs, happy caps, & our signature 72 ounce Guzzler.

All papers are stamped and my check has been cashed. Papers were
filled out by our manager Tito Laguna. Skip Fidget is our opening
headliner. Followed by Mop Head. They have already been paid and
I have over 2,000 t-shirts just waiting for my liquor license

I was told to write you with this information when I called.

Thank you for your assistance

Respectfully,

F.D. Nancy
F.D. Nancy

PALMDALE

a place to call home

January 7, 2010

JAMES C. LEDFORD, JR.
Mayor

TOM LACKEY
Mayor Pro Tem

LAURA BETTENCOURT
Councilmember

MIKE DISPENZA
Councilmember

STEVEN D. HOFBAUER
Councilmember

38300 Sierra Highway

Palmdale, CA 93550-4798

Tel: 661/267-5100

Fax: 661/267-5122

TDD: 661/267-5167

F.D. Nancy
1413-½ Kenneth Rd., #193
Glendale, CA 91201

Re: Liquor License for Something Smells Funny

Dear F.D. Nancy:

We are in receipt of your letter dated January 3, 2010; however, the City does not issue liquor licenses, you must contact the Department of Alcoholic Beverage Control.

However, enclosed are the Business License Application and the Occupancy Review Form that are required in order to have a business in the City of Palmdale.

If you have any questions please contact the Planning Department at 661/267-5200.

Sincerely,

Lynn O'Brien
Administrative Secretary

Enclosures

Auxiliary aids provided for

communication accessibility

upon 72 hours' notice and request.

w w w . c i t y o f p a l m d a l e . o r g

F. D. NANCY (MR)
1413 1/2 Kenneth Rd #193
Glendale, CA 91201

Patient Records
Phoenix Memorial Hospital
1201 S 7th Ave
Phoenix, AZ 85007   19 Apr 2009

Dear Phoenix Hospital,

I was wondering if you could send me my medial records after
treatment at your hospital while visiting Phoenix.

I was there from Feb 2, 2009 thru Feb 7, 2009. for hospital stay.
I had a ladder removed from my head. I was in a construction
accident and was impaled. This is a simple 4 step kitchen ladder
with rubber on each step. It was in my head.

I now need my medical records for insurance purposes. Can you
send?

I believe my doctors name was Dr Marteen Gui or Dr. Marvin Goo or
something like that. (An outstanding emergency room physician!)

Your hospital gave me wonderful treatment I am recovering nicely.
Although my ear continues to flap over (will not stay up, only 1
ear)

I need these medical records for my Insurance Company to properly
assist me.

Thank you for your help and helping others. I am grateful.

Respectfully,

F.D. Nancy

F.D. Nancy (MR)

Date: 4/30/2009

To: Fd Nancy
          1413 1 2 Kenneth Rd 193
          Glendale, AZ 91201

From: Correspondence Coordinator
          Phoenix Memorial Hospital
          2000 West Bethany Home Rd
          Phoenix, AZ 85015

Re: Notice of Facility Closure
          Medical Records Request for Fd Nancy
Ref #:

Dear Fd Nancy:

Phoenix Memorial Hospital shut down as of 6/1/07, therefore, we do not have any
records dated after 5/31/2007. The Urgent Care that is now in it's place is not affiliated
with Abrazo Health Care, it is apart of the Maricopa Integrated Health System.

Sincerely,

Correspondence Coordinator
Health Information Management Department (602)246-5605

Phoenix Baptist Hospital
An Affiliate of Abrazo Health Care

HIM Dept. 5090
2000 W. Bethany Home Road
Phoenix, Arizona 85015

PRESORTED
FIRST CLASS

UNITED STATES POSTAGE
PITNEY BOWES
02 1A $ 00.39
0004340167   MAY 06 20
MAILED FROM ZIP CODE 850

PBH-SR381   DAE-G11   91201

1413 1/2 Kenneth Rd. #193
Glendale, CA 91201

Customer Service Dept.
ALMOND JOY CANDY
c/o Hersheys Candy Co.
Hershey, PA 17033   Nov 17, 2009

Dear Hershy Candy:

I am in the process of marrying a a woman named JOY ALMOND. I met
her through the Pacific Rim Dating Service. She cost me $300. in
tests. She didn't know there was a candy bar with her name
backwards. I took her to the store and she had a good laugh.
Then she was moody the rest of the day. I asked her why she was
moody but she said nothing.

I pried but she sulked. When i unwrap an Almond Joy candy to
enjoy she bares her teeth on me. But i like my Almond Joy. It is
the finest candy out there with the combination of coconut
sprinkles inside.

My relationship with this woman is strained. But what can i do,
Almond Joy? Can you tell me how many calories are in one of your
candy bars? I am getting heavy. I only eat Hershy candy. Do you
still manufacture Jolly Ranchers? That is some candy!

Sincerely,

Ted L. Nancy

Ted L. Nancy

The Hershey Company

December 3, 2009

Mr Ted Nancy
193
1413 1/2 W Kenneth Rd
Glendale, CA 91201-1478

Dear Mr Nancy:

I hope you are enjoying   ALMOND JOY Candy Bar. The nutrition information for this product is:

Serving Size / Calories: 1 bar (1.61 oz)/220

Total Fat: 13 g
Saturated Fat: 8 g
Cholesterol: 0 mg
Sodium: 70 mg
Total Carbohydrates: 26 g
Dietary Fiber: 2g
Sugar: 20 g

We believe that confectionery can be part of a healthy diet. Both chocolate and non-chocolate candies contribute a great deal of enjoyment and satisfaction to eating without being a significant source of calories. As a matter of fact, confectionery products contribute less than 2% of the average adult and child's daily intake of calories. As with all foods, the key to maintaining a healthy diet is to consume confections in moderation and as part of a balanced diet and active lifestyle.

The Hershey Company already offers consumers a variety of product choices and portion sizes to meet their individual lifestyle needs, promotes an active lifestyle, advertises and markets its products responsibly, and most importantly, ensures consumers have the nutrition information they need to make decisions about the role of individual products in their diet.

The vast majority of consumers know that candy is a treat and, like most foods, should be consumed in moderation as part of a balanced diet. The message is not intended to tell consumers what and how much food they should eat. That is entirely up to the individual consumer. The message is only intended to reinforce what is commonly recognized as good nutritional advice.

Your interest in our company is appreciated.

Sincerely,

Robert Lentz
Consumer Representative

Consumer Relations Department
100 Crystal A Drive • PO Box 815 • Hershey, Pennsylvania 17033-0815 • Phone: 1-800-468-1714 • http://www.hersheys.com

1413 1/2 Kenneth Rd. #193
Glendale, CA 91201
ted1nancy1@gmail.com

Jobs Dept.
City of Phoenix
Phoenix City Hall
200 W. Washington St.
Phoenix, AZ 85003   Aug 9, 2009

Dear City Of Phoenix:

I will be moving to Phoenix soon for the moisture and seeking
employment. I was told to write you and you could direct me to
the proper department. I am seeking job information.

I am an expert that can identify ladders. I am a level 5Bjs
trained specialist. I have taught ladders at the Internet junior
college level (in Berlin) I have 3 diplomas signed by officials
with embossed raised seals. I can identify step ladders and
kitchen stools. ·There is a difference! I can tell an aluminum 5
step ladder from a 3 step roof ladder. paint stained ladders are
a specialty and i have written pamphlets on these. Yesterday a
man asked me to show him a wooden ladder. I did. Because of my
standing in the German ladder community I am respected and called
on for professional opinions.

I was told the City of Phoenix has jobs available in the LADDER
SECTOR. Where do I apply? How can I fill out papers? Will you
help me?

Phoenix has the best barbecue in Arizona. I once had a chicken
sandwich there (in 2004) I have had only 1 accident with a
ladder.

I look forward to hearing from you.

Respectfully,

Ted L. Nancy
Ted L. Nancy

Fw: City of Phoenix Feedback Inbox x

laura.neal@phoenix.gov hide details 9:09 AM (1 hour ago)
TEDLNANCY1@gmail.com
Tue, Aug 11, 2009 at 9:09 AM
Fw: City of Phoenix Feedback
phoenix.gov

Hi Ted,

I am not aware of any ladder specialist positions at the City of Phoenix, but I am going to provide you with the steps you need to know in order to apply for positions with the City. Good luck!

The City of Phoenix offers a list of employment opportunities that are available each week and we accept resumes and/or applications only for currently advertised openings. Log on to phoenix.gov/jobs for a complete list of current recruitments. You may also sign up to receive a weekly recruitment listing email at this site.

HOW TO APPLY: You may apply for a position during the recruitment period, which can last for one week up to several weeks/months. All applicants will be evaluated to determine if they meet the minimum requirements of that particular position (as stated on the job announcement). If they do, their name is placed on the eligible list and that list is given to any hiring supervisor who has the authorization to fill their vacancy for that job classification. The list of names is valid for up to 12 months and you need to apply for each of our positions individually.

1. phoenix.gov/jobs
2. Are you a current COP employee? Yes or No
3. Register or log in (first time users need to complete their personal data: name, address, phone, email)
4. Click on the job title of the position you would like to be considered for.
5. Please read the entire job description for important information and tailor your resume to what is being asked for.
6. Apply for the position by uploading a resume or typing in your application information.
7. Answer the questions asked as they are provided by the hiring supervisors and are used as a tool by them.
8. When you are done and want to apply make sure you press **SUBMIT**!

I hope this information helps you, please let me know if I can answer any other questions for you.

Laura Neal
Personnel Analyst II
City of Phoenix Employment Services
(602) 261-8864 (w)
(602) 495-5498 (fax)
---- Forwarded by Laura Neal/PER/PHX on 08/11/2009 09:05 AM ----

1413 1/2 Kenneth Rd. #193
Glendale, CA 91201

FOND (Friends of Neil Diamond)
Box 3357
Hollywood, CA 90028   7/12/9

Dear Neil Diamond Fan Club,

I am a fan of NEIL DIAMOND and want to join ANYTHING about him. I
work in a store that sells diamonds. It is called NEIL DIAMONDS.
The owner's name is NEAL PARMESAN. Coincidentally, NELL DIAMONDS
is his wife. It is a weird world. How do I join the NEIL DIAMOND
FAN CLUB?

Respect,

F. D. Nancy

F.D. Nancy

F.O.N.D. P.O. Box 3357 Hollywood, California 90028

www.neildiamond.com   Friends of Neil Diamond

Dear Friend,

Thank you for your recent inquiry regarding the FRIENDS OF NEIL DIAMOND (FOND) Fan Club. Membership dues are $12.00 for the first year and $6.00 per year to renew. Outside the U.S.A., $16.00 for the first year ($30.00 if you want to receive your new member pack via airmail) and $8.00 per year to renew, in U.S. Dollars only. As a new member you will receive:

> Neil Diamond Tour Program Book
> Several back issues of the FOND newsletter
> FOND membership CARD
> Neil Diamond's biography and discography
> Current year's photo

Once a member, you will receive several newsletters and a new photo each year. Unfortunately membership cannot aid in or guarantee availability of concert tickets or concert information. All tickets must be purchased through local ticket organizations.

As the president of FOND, I welcome you as a new member, as I am sure do all the other devoted FRIENDS. Thank you for your interest. If you would like to join FRIENDS OF NEIL DIAMOND, please send your check or money order payable to FRIENDS OF NEIL DIAMOND to the following address:

> FRIENDS OF NEIL DIAMOND
> P.O. BOX 3357
> HOLLYWOOD CA 90028

We look forward to your membership.

Sincerely,

Jo Michaels

Jo Michaels
President

1413 1/2 Kenneth Rd. #193
Glendale, CA 91201

Information
SHAQUILLE O'NEAL FAN CLUB
CLEVELAND CAVALIERS BASKETBALL TEAM
1 Center Court -
Cleveland, OH 44115-4001   11/30/2009

Dear Cleveland Cavaliers Basketball Team:

I want to join the SHAQUILLE O'NEAL FAN CLUB. I work in a
restaurant called SHAQUILLE O'VEAL. The owner's name is O'NEAL
PICATA.

Also what would be the best way to buy season tickets as i am
moving to Cleveland soon? Do you sell Garden Gnomes?

Thank you.

Respectfully.

F.D. Nancy

F.D. Nancy

mine◯mine

P.O. Box 951840
LAKE MARY, FL. 32795-1840

FD Nancy
1413 1/2 Kenneth Rd #193
Glendale, CA 91201

Member of the SHAQ Network

02 1P
0002371148 APR 19 2010
MAILED FROM ZIP CODE 32746

UNITED STATES POSTAGE
$ 01.05°
PITNEY BOWES

WELCOME TO SHAQ'S OFFICIAL FANCLUB!
THE SHAQ NETWORK.

AS A MEMBER YOU WILL RECEIVE MEMORABILIA AND UPDATE INFORMATION ABOUT SHAQUILLE.

WOULD YOU LIKE TO JOIN THE BIRTHDAY CLUB?
JUST SEND US YOUR BIRTHDATE
(month, day and year please)

#33

UNTIL LATER . . .

SHAQ NETWORK GUIDELINES

1. Membership is open to adults and children of all ages.

2. Membership is valid for as long as the network is in existence.

3. You will remain active as long as you communicate with Shaquille and/or the network staff. There is no limit on the times you write to **SHAQ** or the network. You will always receive an answer.

4. **MEMBERSHIP IS FREE!**

5. **STAY ACTIVE AND TELL A FRIEND!**

    Remember, in your spare time read a book. It will help to expand your mind.

1413 1/2 KENNETH RD.   #193
Glendale, CA 91201
f.d.nancy@lycos.com

Costume Information
Everbest (Qingdao) Company
Room 601, 19 Xiang Gang Xi Road,
Qingdao Shandong
China 266071   8/3/2009

Dear Everbest (Qingdao) Company ,

I am am interested in buying a costume.

I do an act called: OWL CAPONE.

This is me and my owl dressed up like Al Capone with a cigar and a
fedora. We act out the 1920's Chicago beer wars.

I go around the country to fairs and events & cruise ships with my
owl dressed like a gangster and put on a show. "Al" (my owl)
puffs a cigar. (not real) He wears a striped suit and spats on
his feet. I feed him from the buffet.

Do you have tiny gangster costumes?   Smallish spats?

I can show you a photo of Owl Capone if you like. He does look
like Al Capone (or at least like James Caan) Has been mistaken
for the volatile actor.

I look forward to your reply with rates.

Respectfully,

F. D. Nancy

F.D. Nancy (MR)

First　◆Previous　◆Next　　Print　　Reply　　Reply All　　Forward　　Delete　　Spam

Subject	Re:Inquire about Everbest (Qingdao) Compa ny
Sent Date	08-03-2009 8:48:28 PM
From	"hantangfushi" <hantangfushi@tom.com>
To	f.d.nancy@lycos.com
Cc	holidayfashion@tom.com

Dear Mr Nancy,

Glad receiving your enquiry! We do manufacture by pictures and samples. We still don't have an exact view of your mentioned owl capone, so please send us the pictures.

As the gangster costumes and smallish spats, we enclose some of our products for your reference.

Looking forward for our long-term,stable business relations.

Best regards,

Joanna yu.

===

快来和我一起享受TOM免费邮箱吧！看看除了1.5G，还有什么？
===

186

owl Capone in Camel hair
coat & Fedora

owl Capone getting
rough in 1920's swimsuit

owl (looks like James Caan)
with Tommy Gun

Center
Theatre
Group

L.A.'s Theatre Company

3120141421

Glendale, CA 9/201

Kenneth Rd. #193

blabber

"THE EARL OF SANDWICH IS A CRACKPOT."

—EARL OF CHICKEN WRAP,
July 1641

1413 1/2 Kenneth Rd. #193
Glendale, CA 91201

Customer Service
MARKS & SPENCER GIFT SHOPPE
PO Box 288
Warrington
WA5 7WZ   Nov 23, 2009

Dear Marks & Spencer Gift Shoppe,

I have been eating the FAMISHED DWARF FROZEN DINNERS since 1994.
(when i did not eat it).   This is for plus size dwarfs. The
company i usually deal with had their plant shut down for Indian
Mealmoth infestation. Naturally i can't order from them anymore.

I was told your delightful English Gift Shoppe carried this line
for elegant eaters like myself. i weigh 400. There are 2
Famished Dwarf products i currently eat: BIG MANS DWARF FOOD &
HEFTY FATTY DWARF FROZEN DESSERTS.

Can you send me the new price list? I understand Prince Charles
shoppes at your store. Delightful! I may also want a Snuggie.
Which i believe you stock. What are Food Hampers? is it what I
think it is? Do you separate?

Respectfully,

Ted L. Nancy

Ted L. Nancy

**MARKS &
SPENCER**

Retail Customer Services
Chester Business Park
Wrexham Road
Chester
CH4 9GA

Tel: 0845 302 1234
Fax: 0845 303 0170
www.marksandspencer.com

Mr Ted Nancy
1413 1/2 Kenneth Road
#193 Glendale
CA 91201
USA

Our Ref: 1-257166077
10 December 2009

Dear Mr Nancy

Thank you for your letter and for taking an interest in the items that M&S currently sell.

We do stock a large range of fresh and frozen prepared meals but do not currently sell the particular range that you referred to in your letter. We do not currently have any stores in the USA and also do not deliver our food internationally and so I am at a loss to explain how you would be able to get the prepared meals that we do sell. In addition, we also do not stock 'snuggies' and so I am afraid that I am unable to help you locate them in our stores.

During the Christmas period, we are selling food hampers which are boxes or baskets of various luxury food and drink items which can be sent as gifts. These are delivered to customers at home, or there are also some which can be bought directly from our stores. Again, we only deliver these hampers to UK addresses and so I'm afraid that they are not available in the USA.

I am sorry that I cannot help you further at this time but if you do require any further information about our products, please do not hesitate to write to us again.

Thank you again for getting in touch with us.

Yours sincerely

KHoulihan.

Kate Houlihan
Customer Adviser
Retail Customer Services

Marks and Spencer plc
Registered Office:
Waterside House
35 North Wharf Road
London W2 1NW
Registered No. 214436
(England and Wales)

1413 1/2 Kenneth Rd. #193
Glendale, CA 91201

MS. Kate Houlihan
Customer Service
MARKS & SPENCER GIFT SHOPPE
PO Box 288
Warrington
WA5 7WZ   Jan 2, 2010

Dear MS. Houlihan Marks & Spencer Gift Shoppe,

Thank you for answering me and telling me about the Hamper.

I am sorry you do not stock my items. I was given the items as a
gift from my lady friend who lives in Great Britain. Her name is
Lucy. Can we make arraignments for me to ship items to her?

I am looking for the the OLD DWARF FUDDY DUDDY FATTY PATTIES. Do
you carry? they are delicious and we are both long time eaters of
the HUNGRY DWARF FROZEN FOODS line of quality food.

Also...can i order a personalized cake from you that feeds 36? A
sponge cake please with fancy writing on it. (for Lucy)

What about USA delivery? I am being told you now send to the U.S.
Or should i have you delver it to Lucy in England? (weighs 500)

Thank you for your reply on: The cake. Dwarf food.

Respectfully,

Ted L. Nancy
Ted L. Nancy

```
                              F. D. NANCY
                              1413 1/2 Kenneth Rd. #193
                              Glendale, CA 91201




Ticket Info
Ahmanson Theatre
601 W. Temple St.
Los Angeles, CA 90012                        27 Apr 09




DEAR Ahmanson Theater:

I am writing about not receiving my tickets yet to one of your
musicals.

I had purchased 4 tickets to the saucy revue "NOT ON MY DINNER
PLATE YOU WON'T" and have not yet received them.  They were bought
some time ago and the play is coming up rapidly.  I am anxious.

This is for the June 1 performance in the Loge.  I only sit in the
Loge.  Except when I sit in the Mezzanine (or the balcony)  But
only the Loge.  Can you check your Loge seating for:

June 1
4 tickets
"NOT ON MY DINNER PLATE YOU WON'T"

I have the correct paperwork if you need to see.  Could also be
under the name of REV. JUANITA MINCEY, group leader.  Or possibly
under DR. KARL PEACH)  I have gone to past performances at the
Ahmanson and have always been very happy.  Now I have no tickets
to this saucy afternoon revue matinee that was a staple in
Laughlin at the Ginger Belle Hotel.  (I was a platinum copper
delegate)  I was delighted when i heard your theater was re-doing
it into a grand musical.

Please, can you check for me?  Thank you for your reply.


Respectfully,
```

F. D. Nancy

```
F.D. Nancy (MR)
```

Center Theatre Group

L.A.'s Theatre Company

Ahmanson Theatre | Mark Taper Forum | Kirk Douglas Theatre
OFFICES 601 West Temple Street, Los Angeles, CA 90012
CenterTheatreGroup.org

F.D. Nancy
1413 ½ Kenneth Road #193
Glendale, CA 91201

April 28, 2009

Dear F.D. Nancy:

Thank you for your letter. Unfortunately, we do not have a show called "Not on My Dinner Plate You Won't" and we also do not have a show on June 1st. I believe you may have the wrong venue. Please double check your paperwork as no one here has even heard of the show.

If you have any questions please feel free to call 213.628.2772 and an Audience Services Phone Representative will be happy to assist you.

Respectfully Yours,

Alice Chen
Audience Services Assistant Supervisor
Center Theatre Group

```
                              TED L. NANCY
                              1413 1/2 Kenneth Rd. #193
                              Glendale, CA 91201

                              Nov 1, 2008




Reservations
EMBASSY SUITES HOTEL
9801 Airport Blvd.
Los Angeles, CA 90045




Dear Embassy Suites Hotel:

I want to stay at your hotel for one night December 10, 2008.  I
want to check in with my own ice machine.  I have been traveling
with my ice machine since 1996 when I stayed at the Disneyland
Hotel & wrote them a very nice letter.  To date there have been no
incidents.

This ice machine is five feet high and three feet wide.  I can get
it to the room by myself.  I measured your front desk area and I
have 17 inches to maneuver it to the elevator without hitting
anyone.  (If I am careful).

This ice machine DOES NOT drip anymore on the carpet.  The pan is
fixed!  All rust has been removed.  Cracked tray replaced.  And if
it does drip I will bring carpet swatches to replace the dripped
on area.  I have 2 shades of shag.  Avocado and Flonge.  This will
allow me to have fresh ice in the room without having to go in the
hallway.

I have always admired the Embassy Suites Hotel.  They cater to the
traveler, of which I am one.  I like your pool mats.  They are the
finest I have ever laid on.  Even when I turn.  I highly recommend
them.  (If I could)

Please confirm my reservation for December 10th, 2008.  I await my
stay.


Sincerely,
```

Ted L. Nancy

EMBASSY SUITES
HOTELS®

EMBASSY SUITES® HOTEL LAX
INTERNATIONAL AIRPORT NORTH
9801 AIRPORT BOULEVARD
LOS ANGELES, CA 90045

TEL (310) 215-1000
FAX (310) 215-1952 GUEST SVCS
FAX (310) 417-8968 SALES

FOR NATIONWIDE RESERVATIONS
CALL: 1-800-EMBASSY

MR. TED L. NANCY
1413 1/2 Kenneth Rd. #193
Glendale, CA 91201

Nov 5, 2008

Dear Mr. Nancy:

Thank you for inquiring about staying at the Embassy Suites in your letter to us, dated Nov 1, 2008. And thank you for the nice compliments regarding our hotel. It is always delightful to hear such wonderful things regarding our swimming pool mats. At the Embassy Suites we strive hard to make your stay a most enjoyable one. We pride ourselves on that.

In that regard, yes, we can confirm your reservation for one night, checking in Wednesday, December 10th and departing Thursday, Dec 11, 2008.

Regarding checking in with your own ice machine, we have ice machines on the 8th floor, near to the room we have reserved for you. In addition, if you need more ice we can assist you through room service.

However, we at the Embassy Suites want to accommodate our guests in any way we can.

We look forward to your stay with us.

Sincerely,

Paul Verduin
General Manager

196

```
                              F. D. NANCY
                              1413 1/2 Kenneth Rd. #193
                              Glendale, CA 91201




Ticket Info
Ahmanson Theatre
601 W. Temple St.
Los Angeles, CA 90012              5 Aug 2009




Dear Ahmanson Theater:

I ordered tickets awhile ago for one of your musicals and have not
received them.  I bought 6 tickets to the titillating afternoon
revue:  "HEY, I DRINK OUT OF THAT GLASS"

This is for the September 9th performance in the Mezzanine.  I
only sit in the Mezzanine. (Except when I sit in the Loge or the
Balcony) so maybe you can look for them in that seating area.

I have the paperwork if you need to see.  Could also be under the
name of CARLOS FOO.  I have gone to other shows at the Ahmanson
and have been very pleased with the exceptional service and of,
course, customer attention to detail.

Can you help me find my tickets?  Sep 9 is approaching rapidly.
This play ran for 11 months at the Maheenos Indian Casino.  I am
glad it is now at your theater for an even longer run.

I hope you can assist me with my tickets?  I am a platinum gold
circle member.  Thank you, Ahmanson, for caring about your ticket
holders.  Maybe it's under another name.  I have a few.


Respectfully,

F. D. Nancy

F.D. Nancy
```

**Center
Theatre
Group**

L.A.'s Theatre Company

Ahmanson Theatre | Mark Taper Forum | Kirk Douglas Theatre
OFFICES 601 West Temple Street, Los Angeles, CA 90012
CenterTheatreGroup.org

August 11, 2009

Mr. F.D. Nancy
1413 ½ Kenneth Road Suite 193
Glendale, CA 91201

Dear Mr. F.D. Nancy:

Thank you for your recent letter requesting information about your tickets for "Hey, I drink out of that Glass." Unfortunately, we do not have a show with this name playing. Neither could I find it when doing a search for the show name or for the Maheenos Indian Casino on the internet.

We also do not have a platinum gold circle membership and neither the Music Center Founders nor the Development Department at Center Theatre Group were able to find an account for you in their records. (I had them check just in case you had purchased other tickets with a different title for the production.)

You may want to look at your paperwork again to make sure you are contacting the correct venue. On September 9th the only show we have is Steppenwolf's "August: Osage County" which will be running through October 18, 2009. All of our other theatres are in-between shows.

Thank you again for letter. We apologize that we are unable to assist you further.

Respectfully Yours,

Alice Chen
Audience Services Assistant Supervisor
Center Theatre Group

1413 1/2 Kenneth Rd. #193
Glendale, CA 91201

Executive Offices
FARUP SOMMERLAND THEME PARK
Pirupvejen 147, 9493,
Saltum Denmark   NOV 25, 2009

DEAR FARUP SOMMERLAND THEME PARK Denmark.

I am trying to locate my mother. I understand you have an
employee working in your theme park professionally known as:
DYNA THE MIGHTY MITE. (Real first name Gloria.) She is part of
the performing "Squeak Family" of which PEEPO THE WONDER SQUIRT is
her husband.

I believe she works in your performance department. (eats at your
Restaurant; a lot of herring) She is my mother She has a
prominent freckle. She is needed for a family emergency and we
are trying to locate her. She does manatee imitations and plays
the oboe for guests at theme parks. Her catch phrase is: "I
gotta-I gotta-I gotta bad itch on my scalp." Says it a lot in her
act. I believe she is employed by you.

We need to locate her immediately and are having trouble.

I was told to write you with these details.

Can you let me know if my mother is working at your theme park?
Maybe at the Crumb Club.

Thank you, FARUP SOMMERLAND THEME PARK for caring for others and
helping others with people. For others. In matters.

Sincerely,

Ted L. Nancy
Ted L. Nancy

Ted L. Nancy
1413 ½ Kenneth Rd. #193
Glendale, CA 91201
USA

Fårup Sommerland, 02/12/2009

Dear Mr. Nancy

We have received our letter regarding our mother.

Unfortunately we are not able to help you out as we have
never heard about her. We do not have that kind of
performance in our park and all our employees are Danish.
Our park is only open May through August.

I hope you will be successful in finding your mother
somewhere else.

Best regards,
Fårup Sommerland

Jesper H. Jensen

Fårup · Pirupvejen 147 · DK - 9492 Blokhus
Tel +45 98 88 16 00 · Fax +45 98 88 16 20 · www.faarupsommerland.dk

TED L. NANCY
1413 1/2 Kenneth Rd. #193
Glendale, CA 91201
tedlnancy1@gmail.com

Leasing Information
Kringlan, verslunarmistö,
Kringlunni 4-12, 103 Reykjavík,
ICELAND
kringlan@kringlan.is   Jul 9, 2009

Dear KINGLAN Mall Leasing:

I am interested in leasing mall space for my store in Iceland. I
was told to contact you.

I will open EYE BROWSE. This is an eyeglass store that allows for
leisurely browsing. This is not to be confused with EYE .BROWS
which is not us!

You can browse leisurely in my EYE BROWSE store looking at glasses
and frames (and whatever else we have to look at). We are a
discount eye browsing store much, much cheaper (that's 2 muches)
then our * competitors. Eye Browse lets you really take your
time, we encourage it. While Eye Brows are strips of hair over
your eyes. We usually are located in a canvas tent like covering
rather then a cement store. This canvas tent will be set up in
the malls like a kiosk. However while a kiosk is open, our tent
store allows customers to come in. The walls flap a little but
flap noise is kept to a minimum especially with air conditioning.
However, if you prefer I could rent a store with walls. Or any
other store you have vacant. I am open on this (but prefer the
tent)

I am the former owner of RIGAMA ROLLS which was a discount
sandwich roll company that we felt we over expanded and eventually
closed. We were located in the Tent store at many, many malls.

Please direct me as to who I get prices and info from for longtime
leasing. Your mall is highly recommended by certain people. I
will be hiring locally and paying for parking.

Respectfully,

Ted L. Nancy
Ted L. Nancy

Kringlan Shopping Center

Kringlunni 4-12
103 Reykjavík
Iceland

Tel. + 354 568 9200
Fax + 354 568 9572

« Back to "malls/airport"   **Remove label "malls/airport"**   Report spam   Delete   Move to

(no subject)

Sigurjón Örn Þórsson |
Kringlan
tedlnancy1@gmail.com
Mon, Jul 13, 2009 at 3:35 AM

Jul 13 (7 days ago)

Hello Ted

Thank you for showing Kringlan mall your intrest. At the moment there is no vacancy in the mall but I will keep your info on file.

Best regards

Sigurjon Orn Thorsson
General Manager
Kringlan 4-12
103 Reykjavík
Iceland
Tel. +354 517 9000
Fax. +354 517 9010

CINGEGANGEN

0 6. JAN. 2010

1413 1/2 Kenneth Rd. #193
Glendale, CA 91201

Executive Offices
Taunus Wunderland Freizeitpark GmbH
Haus Zur Schanze 1
65388 Schlangenbad Germany

Dec 14, 2009

DEAR Taunus Wunderland Theme Park

I am trying to locate my father. I understand you have an
employee working in your theme park professionally known as:
PEEPO THE WONDER SQUIRT. (Real name Rudy Funch) He is part of
the performing "Squeak Family" of which PIP THE MIGHTY SQUEAK is
no longer involved.

I believe he works in your performance department. (Bungee jumps
in bicycle shorts) He is my father. He has a catfish mustache.
He is needed for a family emergency and we are trying to locate
him. He may also be known as HALF THE MIGHTY PINT and he does
pelican imitations and plays the banjo for guests at theme parks.
His catch phrase is: ""I needa-I needa-I needa an ointment on my
scalp" He says it a lot in his act. I believe he is employed by
you.

We need to locate him immediately and are having trouble.

I was told to write you with these details.

Can you let me know if my father is working at your theme park?
Maybe in the woods wall climbing or tower scrambling.

Thank you, Taunus, for caring for others and helping others with
people. For others. In matters.

Sincerely,

Ted L. Nancy

Schlangenbad bei Wiesbaden
Tel. 06124/40 81   Fax 48 61

Ted L. Nancy

1413 1/2 Kenneth Rd. 193

Glendale

CA 91201 - USA

912013l42l

Freizeitpark GmbH

Haus zur Schanze 1 · D-65388 Schlangenbad
Tel. 06124/4081 · Fax 06124/4861 · www.taunuswunderland.de

Ted L. Nancy

1413 1/2 Kenneth Rd. 193

Glendale

CA 91201 - USA

Sie korrespondieren mit
Mr. Wagner

Datum: 11.1.2010

Ihr Schreiben vom

Unser Gespräch vom

Anbei erhalten Sie

Mit der Bitte um

Very sorry but we do
know him and he
never worked in our
park!
Best rgds

Mit freundlichen Grüßen

204

1413 1/2 Kenneth Rd. #193
Glendale, CA 91201
f.d.nancy@lycos.com

Sales Assistance
Century 21 Fischer Rounds
125 E. Dakota Ave.
Pierre, SD 57501   7/14/2009

Dear Real Estate Company,

Can you please help me find mall space for my store:
REALLY THICK FLOSS.

Please tell me who I contact in your office to help me find store
space in Pierre. You have been highly recommended. Thank you.

I look forward to hearing from you.

Respectfully,

F.D. Nancy

F.D. Nancy (MR)

| First | ↟ Previous | ↡ Next | Print | Reply | Reply All | Forward | Delete | Spam |

Subject	Mall Space Lease
Sent Date	07-15-2009 10:14:11 AM
From	Terry Hipple <thipple@fischerrounds.com>
To	"'f.d.nancy@lycos.com'" <f.d.nancy@lycos.com>

F.D. Nancy:

Regarding your request for someone to contact regarding mall space lease for your store Really Thick Floss, I would encourage you to contact the following:

Pierre Mall
Dee Costello (mall manager)
605-334-6331

PEDCO (our economic development corporation)
Jim Protextor
605-224-6610

Midwest Development (the have rental space in strip type mall)
Glennis Zarecky (one of the owners)
605-224-6345

There may be others that Jim Protextor could advise on, but these are the ones that come to mind first.

Good luck with your search and we hope you are able to set up shop here in Pierre.

Please let them know I gave you there names.

Respectfully,

Terry Hipple
Broker Associate
Century 21 Fischer, Rounds & Assoc.
Cell: 222-9521
Office: 605-224-9223
Fax: 605-224-5831

1413 1/2 Kenneth Rd. #193
Glendale, CA 91201

Glennis Zarecky,
Midwest Development of Pierre
740 E Sioux Ave, #110,
Pierre, SD 57501   July 15, 2009
information@zmidwest.com

Dear Glennis Zarecky of Pierre,

Terry Hipple has suggested I contact you regarding leasing mall
space for my store: REALLY CLOGGED STRAWS

I am opening soon in the Kringlan Mall in Iceland (Reykjavík) and
also want to lease in Pierre, South Dakota.

Terry Hipple is one of the finest people in the real estate
business. He is a credit to the community of Pierre. I look
forward to leasing from you at his suggestion. Can you help me?

Thank you for your reply.   (Your email does not work)

Respectfully,

F. D. Nancy

F.D. Nancy (MR)

```
                              F. D. NANCY
                              1413 1/2 Kenneth Rd. #193
                              Glendale, CA 91201




Ticket Info
Ahmanson Theatre
601 W. Temple St.
Los Angeles, CA 90012                   18 Dec 2009




Dear Ahmanson Theater:

I ordered tickets awhile ago for one of your musicals and have not
received them yet.  I bought 9 tickets to the hilarious afternoon
revue:  "HEY, I EAT WITH THAT MOUTH"

This is for the January 21st performance in the Orchestra.  (I
always sit in the Orchestra)

I have the paperwork if you need to see.  Could also be under the
name of CHET POCK.  He is our group associate,.  I have gone to
other shows at the Ahmanson and have been very pleased with the
exceptional service and of, course, customer attention to detail.

Can you help me find my tickets?  January 21, 2010 is approaching
rapidly.  This play ran for 59 weeks at the Cahungas Indian
Casino.  I am glad it is now presented at your theater for our
enjoyment.

Can you assist me with my tickets?  I am a diamond gold preferred
silver anniversary member.  Thank you, Ahmanson, for caring about
your ticket holders.


Respectfully,

F. D. Nancy

F.D. Nancy
```

Center Theatre Group

L.A.'s Theatre Company

Ahmanson Theatre | Mark Taper Forum | Kirk Douglas Theatre
OFFICES 601 West Temple Street, Los Angeles, CA 90012
CenterTheatreGroup.org

21 December 2009

F.D. Nancy
1413 ½ Kenneth Road, #193
Glendale, CA 91201

Hello,

We received your letter regarding your purchase of a show called *Hey I Eat With That Mouth* for a performance on January 21, 2010. Unfortunately that is not a production that the Ahmanson Theatre is presenting or has any affiliation with.

Truthfully, I've not heard of that show so I don't know where it is playing or how to assist you.

During January we will be running the musical *Mary Poppins* at the Ahmanson and *Palestine, New Mexico* at the Mark Taper Forum (next to the Ahmanson). By any chance do you have tickets to one of those productions?

Respectfully,

Scott Taylor
Audience Services Supervisor
213/628-2772

```
                              F. D. NANCY
                              1413 1/2 Kenneth Rd. #193
                              Glendale, CA 91201


Mr. Scott Taylor
Ticket Info
Ahmanson Theatre
601 W. Temple St.
Los Angeles, CA 90012              26 Dec 2009



Dear Mr. Scott Taylor Ahmanson Theater:

Thank you for writing me with information on a play I have tickets
for.  Now I am informed the play is called:

"KEEP THAT OUT OF GARY'S NOSTRIL!"

I believe it stars Dom Deluise & Koko Kardashian in a ribald
afternoon revue. (Most recently it was at the Bazoomas Indian
Casino.)  .

I Got my letter with parking instructions.  My confirmation # is
B-71-C9. Parking level 3.  It has the Ahmanson name on it &
address for Jan 29, 2010.  I paid $62.50 each.  Our group leader
is RALPH HEM.  Can you check for me when I will receive the actual
tickets?

And yes!  I would love to See "MARY TODD POPPINS IN MEXICO"

I believe it was mostly recently at the Lincoln Theater in
Springfield.  How do i arrange tickets?

I look forward to hearing from you on:
A.  My tickets for  "KEEP THAT OUT OF GARY'S NOSTRIL!"
B.  New ticket information for "MARY TYLER POPPINS IN NEW MEXICO"

I am a silver club copper zinc member with Platnimum privileges.

Thank you,
```

F.D. Nancy

F.D. Nancy

1413 1/2 Kenneth Rd. #193
Glendale, CA 91201
f.d.nancy@lycos.com

Iceland Tourism Board
Laugavegur 26
101 Reykjavík Iceland   July 26, 2009
iceland@nordicvisitor.com

Dear Iceland Tourism Board,

Can you please tell me how I can request an honor for a person who
has relentlessly promoted your fine country? I am talking about
TORRY HIPPO. How can I recommend him to be glorified in Iceland. I
want to esteem Torry Hippo for being an outstanding messenger of
your wonderful country. He is constantly sounding the trumpet for
Iceland. (and what it means to buy the products of Iceland and
visit their food courts) What is the process for this?

A plaque?
Commendation?
Torry Hippo Day in the mall?

Please write me and tell what the paperwork process is for this.
TORRY HIPPO DAY in the Kringlan Mall in Iceland (Reykjavík) sounds
awfully good to me. I look forward to your reply. Iceland is truly
the land of hospitable people.

Respectfully,

F.D. Nancy

Subject	RE: Bestow Honor Question
Sent Date	07-27-2009 8:35:33 AM
From	"Iceland - Nordic Visitor" <iceland@nordicvisitor.com>
To	"FRED NANCY" <f.d.nancy@lycos.com>

Dear Fred,

I think you got a wrong adress for the tourist board their e-mail adress is upplysingar@icetourist.is.

Kind regards,

Jón Sigurður Ingason
Operations Manager
NORDIC VISITOR - Iceland
Laugavegur 26,
101 Reykjavík,
Iceland
Tel: +354 578 2080
Direct: +354 578 2083
Fax: +354 511 2443
jonsi@nordicvisitor.com
www.icelandvisitor.com

**Nordic Visitor - An Unforgettable Travel Experience**
www.nordicvisitor.com

Certificate of Achievement

The International Fabricare Institute commends

TORRY NIPPLE **Cleaners**

for achieving and maintaining a high standard

of excellence in *REAL ESTATE* solvent quality.

February 6, 2007

Rd. #193
11201

is EVERYONE
still out
tHERE?
lEt ME KnoW

"Both The Earl Of Sandwhich &
The Earl Of Chicken Wrap
Will Beg Me For Help One Day."

—THE EARL OF LAP BAND,
AUGUST 16s7

1413 1/2 Kenneth Rd. #193
Glendale, CA 91201

Show Information
TREASURE ISLAND HOTEL & CASINO
3300 S. Las Vegas Blvd.
Las Vegas, NV 89109   Dec 26, 2009

DEAR Treasure Island Hotel & Casino,

I am interested in buying tickets for your show :

"LEAVE GARY'S FEET OUT OF THIS!"

This is the afternoon provocative revue that has played at the
Kazumbas Indian Casino for 120 weeks and now i understand you are
presenting it. Wonderful! It stars Kaka Kardashian and David
Carradine.

4 tickets please for the Feb 22, 2010 show.

I also would need 3 rooms for that period. How much? Is there a
show-room rate?

Treasure island is a wonderful Las vegas hotel. I have eaten at
your Kahunaville Restaurant to complete satisfaction. Your
Calypso Calamari is UNBELIEVABLE!. Granny loves it and she hates
octopus, squid and 8 legged sea creatures.

Also do you have a wedding chapel? I may marry Tayshon.

Thank you for your reply. I visit there many times and will
continue to do so.

Sincerely,

F.D. Nancy

TREASURE ISLAND
Las Vegas

Treasure Island Hotel & Casino
3300 S. Las Vegas Blvd.
Las Vegas, NV 89109

F.D. Nancy
1413 ½ Kenneth Rd. #193
Glendale, CA 91201

Jan. 7, 2010

Thank you for your letter inquiring about Treasure Island in Las Vegas.

Treasure Island has been the home to Cirque Du Soleil's MYSTERE show for the past 16 years, and will be delighting audiences for years to come. Unfortunately, we are not hosting a show called, "LEAVE GARY'S FEET OUT OF THIS!" We do not have any information as to when or where this is playing. As for room rates, we can give you the most current and up-to-date pricing over the phone at 1-800-944-7444 or by visiting our website at www.treasureisland.com.

Thank you for being a loyal guest to our hotel, and we look forward to seeing you again. There are many new and exciting things going on at our property and welcome you to give us a call for more information at 1-800-944-7444

Best Regards,
Dan Malo
Treasure Island Guest Relations

217

1413 1/2 Kenneth Rd. #193
Glendale, CA 91201

Dan Malo, Guest Relations
TREASURE ISLAND HOTEL & CASINO
3300 S. Las Vegas Blvd.
Las Vegas, NV 89109   Jan 30, 2010

Dear Guest Relations .

Thank you for writing me with Play information i thought I had. I
was mistaken as to the name of the play. It is called:

"LET GO OF GARY'S TOES"

I was completely turned around and got my information wrong.
Also. I am NOT a diamond gold preferred silver anniversary
member. I am a Platinum gold sodium member with Silver Chai
copper inlay privileges, not zinc.

This play is definitely at your hotel, Treasure Island, in Las
Vegas. Probably the nicest place I ever stayed, ate, fell asleep,
and gambled at. And that includes the Mayoyo Indian Casino in
Panyani. You should be proud of this hotel & Casino. I am.

The play is running March 22, 2010, not February 22 and it stars
Ozzie Nelson & Tito Peunte.

Can you let me know anything?

Sincerely,

F.D. Nancy

F.D. Nancy

560 N. Moorpark Rd. Apt #236
Thousand Oaks, CA 91360

Special Promotions
ARMOUR FRESH MEATS
PO Box 470
Nampa, ID 83561

Dear Armour Meats:

I want to take a 59 foot bolonga by 22 foot bolonga on the plane
with me. Can you make? Will it fit in the overhead bin? (I
still have my luggage too)

This is for my Bologna Club. I need this bologna to arrive in one
piece. Southwest Fun Jet C Group Boarding.

I can't put it in baggage. I think a hot bologna in a hot plane
in the hot sun is not such a good idea. Huh?

Hey, what time is it there in Nampa? It's 3 o'clock here. Please
let me know how much this special order boloney is. I have my own
roll. (poppyseed)

Sincerely,

Ted L. Nancy
Meat Chair Committee

ARMOUR FRESH MEAT COMPANY

P.O. BOX 470
NAMPA, IDAHO 83653
AREA CODE 208-466-4627

Ted L. Nancy
Meat Chair Committee
560 No. Moorpark Road #236
Thousand Oaks, CA 91360

Dear Mr. Nancy;

The Nampa plant slaughters and processes beef for the retail markets.

I'm sorry to say that we do not make bologna or any ready to eat items
at this plant. Our primary products are butcher block beef cuts and
trimmings for ground beef.

I think that you may have the measurements wrong. A bologna 59 feet by
22 feet would weigh 60,000 lbs.

We wish you luck.

Sincerely,

Dwayne Evanson
Human Resource Manager

1413 1/2 Kenneth Rd. #193
Glendale, CA 91201
f.d.nancy@lycos.com

Administration
CAMBODIA TOURIST BOARD
#262 Monivong Blvd,
Khan Daun Penh, Phnom Penh,
Kingdom of Cambodia
info@tourismcambodia.com   Aug 15, 2009

Dear CAMBODIA TOURISM OFC ,

What a pleasure it is to write to you and praise one of your
citizens of Cambodia. I would like to single out a citizen of
your country for what i consider to be a great act to me. I have
singled him out here in Glendale. He told me his name was Bineesh
Chong. Can you find him and tell him i would like to donate money
to the peoples of Cambodia for what he did.

I had an incident and this courages young man Chong came to my
distress.

Incident: I pulled a barrel of shellack onto me by mistake while
answering a cell phone call. I was COMPLETELY ENCASED IN VARNISH.
mr. "Bineesh" poked a hole in my mouth with his bic pen for me to
breathe. Then he placed me in a barrel of goo swabee which he
said would soften me. (he called it Gixm or gimoo) Then Mr
Bineesh Chong. carried me around over his head to get circulation
in my limbs. BINEEESH CHONG IS A STUPENDOUS CAMBODIAN!!!

I want to leave a large donation to your country for this act of
what I consider beyond and above and to the complete top of what
is called for in the beyond & above called for world. If this was
real estate he would be in the platinum gold circle class. (of
which I am in) Can you let me know:

Bineesh Chong was praised and a certificate may be issued
My large donation will be accepted (can make it to a Cambodia
cause)

I look forward to your reply.

With respect for your peoples,

F. D. Nancy
F.D. Nancy

First | ↟Previous | ↡Next | Print | Reply | Reply All | Forward | Delete | Spam

Subject	Re: Praise Citizen
Sent Date	08-16-2009 3:07:12 AM
From	"info TC" <info@tourismcambodia.com>
To	"FRED NANCY" <f.d.nancy@lycos.com>

Dear F.D. Nancy

Please take a flight to Cambodia, then there will alot of opportunities for you to make any donations.

Regards

JACK - Director of Marketing and Promotion Department

Tourism Cambodia - The official Travel and Tourist Information Center
#262D, Monivong blvd, Phnom Penh, Camnbodia.
Tel: +(855 23) 212221 / 218585 Fax:+(855 23) 222801 Email: info@tourismcambodia.com
Website: www.tourismcambodia.com

Certificate of Achievement

The International Fabricare Institute commends

~~TOBBY NIBBLE~~ **BINEESH CHONG** Cleaners

for achieving and maintaining a high standard

of e **UNSHELLACKING** *AL ESTATE* solvent quality.

February 6, 2007

223

```
                                     1413 1/2 Kenneth Rd. #193
                                     Glendale, CA 91201
```

```
Entertainment Tickets
MONTE CARLO HOTEL
3770 Las Vegas Boulevard South
Las Vegas, NV 89109                          Jan 16, 2010
```

Dear Monte Carlo Hotel :

Can you please help me? I want to change the seating on my
tickets for your afternoon show:

"GARY WENT BERSERK AND TORE UP A LAUNDROMAT"

This is for Feb 19, 2010. This is the lighthearted European
comedy romp starring Sergio Valente & Sebastian Cabot. With a
special appearance by Kchuck Kardashian.

I received tickets from you and my check for $122.00 was cashed.
I was told if I had to make changes to write you. I am afraid my
seats are too far back and I cannot get up that steep of a
walkaway as I'll slide back. When i called they said to write
with my info. There are 4 in our group including team leader
Boniva Rodriguez.

Thank you. The Monte Carlo is one of the finest hotels and we
always visit and eat and gamble when we are in Las Vegas monthly.
Surprisingly two in our group is named Monte & Carlo. Your Aqua
Dragon Noodle Restaurant and your BBQ pork buns is a treat for our
group! Everyone yums 'em up. We will continue to do so and look
forward to a wonderful matinee performance of this afternoon
whimsical German play.

I look forward to better seats. I am a gold standard Monte Carlo
Players member with silver platinum Venti card club rewards.

Respectfully

F. D. Nancy
F.D. Nancy

                                     STILL WAITING FOR REPLY!
```
224
```

TED L. NANCY
560 No. Moorpark Rd.   Apt #236
Thousand Oaks, CA 91360

Sep 6, 1999

Customer Service Dept.
JIMMY DEAN SAUSAGES
8000 Centerview Parkway # 400
Cordova, TN 38018

Dear Jimmy Dean Meat Co.,

I am a long time eater of your "Jimmy Dean Tastefuls." This is
the Oreos, ham, and Fritos combination. I eat it a lot. Hail
Jimmy Dean! It's a midnight snack to many of us here without
having to go to the vending machine after a bowlful. Jimmy, you
spoke to me with your Tastefuls. I heard you loud & clear. I see
your vision. I am a believer! Hail Jimmy Dean! Hare Krishna
Rama Rama!

A foreign clerk told me of your new snack called "JIMMY DEAN'S IN
BETWEENS." These are between meal snacks. I believe it is mashed
potatoes, Brachs bridge mix, and pie filling. I want it!

Jimmy Dean is the best singer and sausage maker out there. Big
Bad John!

Just wanted you to know I got a mouth full of Tasefuls now. How
do i get it out? Mouthwash won't do it. I taste a lot of ham.

Thank you. I look forward to my reply.

Sincerely,

Ted L. Nancy

Ted L. Nancy

JD Jimmy Dean Foods

Division of Sara Lee Corporation
8000 Centerview Parkway., Suite 400 • Cordova, Tennessee U.S.A. 38018-7927
901-753-1600

September 14, 1999

Mr. Ted L. Nancy
560 No. Moorpark Rd.
Apt #236
Thousand Oaks, CA 91360

Dear Mr. Nancy,

Thank you for contacting Jimmy Dean expressing your satisfaction with Jimmy Dean
Tastefuls. Your kind comments let us know that our continued efforts are appreciated. I
am sorry to inform you that the Jimmy Dean Tastefuls! have been discontinued and we
do not have a product called Jimmy Dean's In Between's. If you do find a product like
this please send us the wrapper so we can check this product out.

From the beginning we have worked very hard to make the very best products possible.
We buy only the best ingredients and prepare them carefully. Our goal is to produce a
fresh, wholesome product that pleases you and your family.

In this hurried world we often forget the importance of a simple thank you. Please
believe us when we say we are most thankful for customers such as you. Please accept
the enclosed coupon for your next purchase of any Jimmy Dean brand product while we
continue our efforts to provide you with products of the quality you expect.

Sincerely,

Linda Fuller
Consumer Affairs Representative

1413 1/2 Kenneth Rd. #193
Glendale, CA 91201

Customer Service Dept.
JIMMY DEAN SAUSAGES
c/o Sara Lee Consumer Affairs
P.O. Box 756
Neenah, WI 54957-0756   26 Apr 2009

Dear Jimmy Dean Meat Co.,

I wrote to you in 1999 and you sent me a coupon for some Jimmy
Dean Sausage Biscuits. (It's me, Ted L. Nancy. Sometimes i go by
Fred or F.D.) I just got around to eating these biscuits (after
picking them up in March 2000) Wow did I NOT feel good. I had
some Jimmy Dean Trots. I sat on the Big Bad John. Woowee!

Is this OK? I am fine now. I had a wash cloth on my head for a
week. (took it off at work but then put it back on again at
night)

i looked on the internet and they say frozen food can stay for
years. They use it in space. That's why I ate these sausage
biscuits. I have no problems. I just want to know how long this
stuff really stays.

Thank you. I look forward to my reply.

Sincerely,

F.D. Nancy
F.D. Nancy

Ted

Sara Lee Consumer Affairs
P O Box 756
Neenah, WI 54957

Bakery   1.800.323.7117
Foodservice   1.800.261.4754
Meats   1.800.328.2426
Senseo   1.866.473.6736

May 4, 2009

M/M F D Nancy
1413 1/2 W KENNETH RD # 193
GLENDALE, CA 91201-1478

Dear M/M Nancy:

Thank you for contacting Sara Lee® with your questions, comments. We guarantee our products to the expiration date on the package. We would not recommend consuming products that are past the date. Enclosed a complimentary coupons for you next Jimmy Dean purchase.

We truly value you as a customer and as always, we will continue to produce superior quality products that meet your expectations.

Sara Lee® Consumer Affairs

Enclosures:
JD99 - (1)

ref. #2356007

F. D. NANCY
1413 1/2 Kenneth Rd. #193
Glendale, CA 91201

Customer Service Dept.
JIMMY DEAN SAUSAGES
Sara Lee Consumer Affairs
P.O. Box 756
Neenah, WI 54957-0756   May 11, 2009

Dear Jimmy Dean Sausage People: ·

Thank you for the coupon for BREAKFAST BOWLS. I just ate a ton of
the stuff and staggered to the mens room. My eyes flew around
like pinwheels. Wowwowwow!

Hey! I just heard about new "JIMMY DEANS I CAN'T FIT INTO MY
JEANS". This is the lunch combination of Country gravy, Funyons,
baking chocolate, hummus, creme de menthe. I need this. Now!

My question: Is anyone checking this stuff out over there? All
these food combinations together? Any inspections going on i
should now about? I mean they got to be from different places. I
once heard of a fast food restaurant where a customer was eating
and found an entire person in a baked potato. (he was missing a
finger)

Jimmy Dean is my favorite freezer food. I stack 'em & pack 'em
into me. Send me more coupons. I truly love this food.

Yea Jimmy Dean!

F. D. Norey

F.D. Nancy (MR)

Sara Lee Consumer Affairs   Bakery   1.800.323.7117
PO Box 756   Foodservice 1.800.261.4754
Neenah, WI 54957   Meats   1.800.328.2426
                                Senseo   1.866.473.6736

May 20, 2009

Ms. F D Nancy
1413 1/2 W KENNETH RD # 193
GLENDALE, CA 91201-1478

Dear Ms. NANCY:

It was a pleasure speaking with you today.   We appreciate that you took the time to contact us.

As we discussed, Sara Lee® is committed to providing our customers with the highest quality products. Sara Lee® firmly believes in the importance of product quality and food safety. We endeavor to see that all products meet the highest standards. We are genuinely concerned when there is a problem or when a product does not meet our consumer's expectations. We have a responsibility to you and to our other customers to properly investigate any such occurrence and we take that responsibility seriously.

In addition, Sara Lee® has rigid quality standards. Our manufacturing facility operates under strict compliance with local, state and federal laws and regulations as well as our own requirements. Our raw ingredient suppliers, all of whom are highly reputable, are required to perform several inspections before shipping the ingredients to us.

We truly value you as a customer and want to assure you that we are committed to manufacturing the highest quality products. We believe in our products and have enclosed complimentary coupons to be used towards your next Sara Lee® purchase. We are confident that your next purchase will meet your expectations. We recommend you use these products by the date shown. If past the use by date, please disacrd the product. If you have any other questions or comments, please contact us at 1-800-323-7117.

Sincerely,

Consumer Affairs Representative
Sara Lee® Consumer Affairs

Enclosures:
JD99 - (3)

ref. #2373609

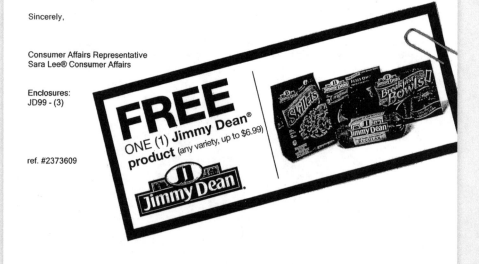

TED L. NANCY
1413 1/2 Kenneth Rd. #193
Glendale, CA 91201
TEDLNANCY1@Gmail.com

Information
E FINANCIAL LIFE INSURANCE   22 May 2009

Dear Insurance Co:

I am looking for life and other insurance. I have a valuable
collection of Pest Strips that need to be insured and I need life
insurance as I trust no one. These were pest strips that were
used to remove bugs from screen doors. (There are mites in some
of them. I have 240 of them. 2 Shell No Pest Strips. Rare!)

How much to insure?   I need life insurance as others may want
this collection.

I am in the process of relocating my collection to a Museum in
Pennsylvania. And I want to insure it. I know insurance can be
costly but what if I lose these pest strips and old air
deodorizers? Huh? What is worth more then? The loss of my
collection and me being inconsolable or some money?

Please tell me who I contact to discuss this very valuable
collection and how I insure it?

My collection will be stored in Modesto until it is moved to the
museum. You have been highly recommended by people in the
licorice community. Thank you. I eagerly await your reply. Call
me Fred. Many do.

Sincerely,

Ted L. Nancy
Ted L. Nancy

Fred, Life insurance quote request

Scott McCoy <scott@mccoyteam.com>   **Fri, May 22, 2009 at 8:32 AM**
Reply-To: scott@mccoyteam.com
To: "TED L. NANCY" <tedlnancy1@gmail.com>

Hi Ted,

We are a life insurance broker. I can provide you with the lowest rates
available for life insurance.
We do not handle insurance for the pest strips.

Please give me a call.

Sincerely,

Scott
========================
Scott McCoy
Life Insurance Specialist
Efinancial
Scott@MccoyTeam.com

TED L. NANCY
1413 1/2 Kenneth Rd. #193
Glendale, CA 91201
TEDLNANCY1@Gmail.com

MR. SCOTT MCCOY
E FINANCIAL LIFE INSURANCE   22 May 2009
scott@mccoyteam.com

Dear Scott,

Thank you for getting back to me so promptly. In this day and age
of people that do not care. You have shown that: You care! I
will note that in an appropriate folder and copy those that need
it. Now down to:

My insurance needs.

As I have recently come into money from a ladder accident and
would like to purchase LIFE INSURANCE maybe you can help. I do
not trust my companion so I should take out this insurance.
However this PEST CONTROL STRIP collection is valuable. She wants
it as I have noticed her eyeing it.

Can I insure this under a HOMEOWNERS POLICY? It's the core of our
problems. Have you ever seen "Double Indemnity" with Fred
MacMurray and Barbara Stanwick? I DO NOT TRUST THIS WOMAN. WATCH
THIS MOVIE!!! She will take these Pest Control Strips. (Including
the 2 Shell No Pest Strips. Rare!)

So now how can we get me some insurance for:

Life
Homeowners.

I have never had insurance before. Thank you for caring about the
needs of others.

Respectfully,

Ted L. Nancy
(Fred)   Fred

P.S. Am also getting quotes from other Insurance Companys.

233

YOUR QUOTE REQUEST   INSURANCE X

Olson Financial Services to me

Hello,

show details Apr 6

Thank you for requesting a quote.

When given the opportunity, we find that the first quote you receive, is not always the lowest.

To provide you with an accurate quote, we pre-underwrite
We then match this with ALL COMPANIES and find

At your earliest convenie

I work for you!

~ Kim
Kim L. Olson, LUTCF
27 Year Insurance Agent
Employer Benefit Services

Your Information Request To Prudential

Intro_Admin@prudential.com <Intro_Admin@prudential.com>
To: "TED L. NANCY" <TEDLNANCY1@gmail.com>, "TED L. NANCY" <Intro_Admin@prudential.com>
Reply | Reply to all | Forward | Print | Delete | Show original

Fri, May 22, 2009 at 3:17 PM

Dear Fred,

Recently, you requesting a life insurance quote online. It is likely that you are no
beginning to receive calls from all over the country from agents interested in taki
care of your needs. Many of these agents are not local but they do have a
nonresident insurance license and can sell you a policy. The true question is do
want to purchase a policy from someone who can sit down with you and your fa
to answer your questions or is a voice on the phone sufficient to accommodate y
needs? Simply do you wish to work with a truly local agent or is someone calling
another state advertising themselves as local good enough? Most often the prod
lines and insurance companies are identical the prices are the same; however th
level of service is greatly different.

Life Insurance is absolutely the easiest, most affordable way to replace your inc
u die. It can provide you with the peace of mind knowing your family wi
today and in the future. Whether you are currently insured or
w Insurance plans that could easily save you mone
and your loved ones around the kitchen tab
e I look forward to helping you establish a li
you.

TAE KIM
TAE.KIM@PRUDENTIAL.COM

ear TED L. NANCY,

e have received your online request for information about Prudential insurance products and
will be happy to help you.

r request has been assigned to the local Prudential agent listed above.

Quot
ca.rr.com

Hi,
I e-mailed your quote on 5-28-09.
When I call you, the answer machine always comes on, as before.
If you have any questions or would like to discuss this, contact me anytime.

~ Kim
Kim L. Olson, LUTCF
27 Year Insurance Agent
Pre-Tax business & Financial Services

TED L. NANCY
1413 1/2 Kenneth Rd. #193
Glendale, CA 91201
TEDLNANCY1@Gmail.com

Kim Olson
OLSON LIFE INSURANCE   27 May 2009

Dear Kim Olson of Olson Life Insurance.

Thank you for helping me with my life insurance needs. Since i
was in an accident recently my companion Phyllis Dietrichson
handles all paperwork as I am recovering from a ladder -
refrigerator incident. I will be taking a train in to meet her as
it is easier for me to get around. Phyllis will meet us at the
train station when i arrive which is easy for me if this Ok as I
am wearing a cast on my right leg and on crutches. So I don't
want to hobble around too much with cars and taxies. Can you give
me a quote so I can analyze figures. Thank you for your reply,

Sincerely,

Ted L. Nancy
Ted L. Nancy

1.25M 10-15-20 INSURANCE x

Olson Financial Services   hide details **May 28**

TEDLNANCY1@gmail.com
Thu, May 28, 2009 at 3:22 PM
1.25M 10-15-20
ca.rr.com

Great to hear from you,
You didn't mention the amount of insurance to quote so I looked up your
request and used the $1.25M.
Hope you recover from your accident quickly.
Any questions, contact me anytime.

~ Kim
Kim L. Olson, LUTCF
27 Year Insurance Agent
Pre-Tax business & Financial Services

TED L. NANCY
1413 1/2 Kenneth Rd. #193
Glendale, CA 91201
TEDLNANCY1@Gmail.com

Tae H. Kim, CLTC, CMFC
Representative
Prudential Life Insurance   13 July 2009

Dear Tae H. Kim, Prudential Life Insurance,

Sorry for the delay in responding. I am recovering with a cast on
my left leg that makes it hard to concentrate. Did i say left
leg? It is the right leg I have a cast on.

I am considering your quote but i will probably need more
coverage. Maybe double. My companion Phyllis Dietrichson wants
me to take out more life insurance. She will handle all life
insurance signings. can we arrange? When we meet at train
station she will blink her lights twice and honk the horn. She
and this Walter Neff fella. He was once with Pacific All Risk and
their top salesman. He is now quite old and out of the business.
I don't know what he babbles about. That is why i need to talk to
you, a professional to get this insurance going.

I am not a smoker. (2nd hand smoke?) how many signatures do you
need? I still have rivets in my head from this slip and fall
refrigerator accident. What is the indemnity here?

Thank you, Tae H. Kim, for being so understanding and dealing with
those that may need a little more time in this. What is next?

Respectfully,

Ted L. Nancy

Ted, Updated Life Insurance Quotes INSURANCE X

Scott McCoy
TED L. NANCY
Scott McCoy

scott@mccoyteam.com
"TED L. NANCY"
<tedlnancy1@gmail.com>
Mon, Jul 13, 2009 at 1:44 PM
RE: Ted, Updated Life
Insurance Quotes

hide details Jul 13 (6 days ago)

Ted,

I need to speak with you over the phone to ask a few questions about your health and family history.

I will then be able to access what you qualify for an give you a more accurate estimate of cost.

We will complete the application over the phone. It will only take about 10-15 minutes.

We will then send a medical examiner to your home at no cost to you. They will take your blood pressure, a vile of blood, weigh you and measure your height.

The process will take 3-8 weeks once your medical exam is complete.

I have tried to call on several occasions but no one ever answers the phone. Please call me

Scott

Life insurance info you requested INSURANCE X

tae.kim@prudential.com
TED L. NANCY
tae.kim@prudential.com
tae.kim@prudential.com
TED L. NANCY
tae.kim@prudential.com
"TED L. NANCY"
<tedlnancy1@gmail.com>
Wed, Jul 15, 2009 at 4:58
PM
Re: Life insurance info
you requested
prudential.com

hide details Jul 15 (4 days ago)   Reply

Dear Ted,

Please let me know when we can discuss your life insurance needs. We need to set an appointment for an in person meeting. We can meet at a Starbuck's Coffee, next to your house. Please let me know when you can meet in the next week or two and the location of the Starbuck's you would like to meet. Do you have a cell phone?

Best regards,
Tae-

TED L. NANCY
1413 1/2 Kenneth Rd. #193
Glendale, CA 91201
TEDLNANCY1@Gmail.com

MR. SCOTT MCCOY
E FINANCIAL LIFE INSURANCE   20 July 2009
scott@mccoyteam.com

Dear MR. SCOTT MCCOY,

Scott. Listen to me. I am in a full body cast and crutches from
an accident. I fell into a barrel of shellack by mistake
answering a cell phone call. I was COMPLETELY ENCASED IN VARNISH.
Bineesh Chong poked a hole in my mouth with his bic pen for me to
breathe. Then he placed me in a barrel of goo swabee which he
said would soften me. (he called it Gixm or gimoo) Then Mr
Bineesh Chong carried me around over his head to get circulation
in my limbs. BINEEESH CHONG IS A STUPENDOUS CAMBODIAN!!

I can't be weighed now or give blood at my home. Or go to
Starbucks. (Although i do like their frappee.) Phyllis and
Walter Neff are having an affair. Neff's boss, Barton Keyes,
knows what is going on. He runs Pacific All Risk. He heard Neff
tell the whole story into a Dictaphone. Neff told Keyes he is
going to Mexico.

I can't have anyone weigh me now. The cast alone weighs 60
pounds. Starbucks is out of the question. I can't get thorough
the door, let alone sit there. How about Coffee Bean?

I need insurance now! A policy for over 2 million WITHOUT Phyllis
Dietrichson as the beneficiary. Barton Keyes adjusted my wig
netting once.

So...when can we finalize this policy for this insurance? I am
ready. What did we ever decide about the Pest Strip collection?
Let me know what is a good time for you.

Sincerely,

Ted L. Nancy
Ted L. Nancy

WEIGH ME AT HOME

Scott McCoy <scott@mccoyteam.com>
Reply-To: scott@mccoyteam.com
To: "TED L. NANCY" <tedlnancy1@gmail.com>

Mon, Jul 20, 2009 at 4:31 PM

Ted,

It is not possible to get you a 2 million dollar policy without a medical exam plus your current condition.

How long were your hospitalized from your accident?

Did you have to have surgery?

The only option at this time would be a non-medical policy (no medical exam).
I would have to investigate further to see if you could qualify.

The most you would be able to get would be $250,000 - $300,000. Are you interested?

We only sell life insurance so I would not be able to help you with the pest strips.

Scott

F.D. NANCY (MR)
1413 1/2 Kenneth Rd. #193
Glendale, CA 91201 USA

PRESIDENT DR.H. SUSILO BAMBANG YUDHOYONO
STATE SECRETARIAT
THE REPUBLIC OF INDONESIA
Jl. Veteran No 18
Jakarta 10110 Indonesia   12/11/2009

Dear PRESIDENT Dr.H. Susilo Bambang Yudhoyono .

Just a note to say that you are the best President of a foreign
country I have ever seen. Indonesians in the U.S. want you to
succeed. I admire and respect what you have done for ALL People.
So do ALL members of our mens group that is made up of
Indonesians. There are 72 of us. We admire Indonesia and what it
means.

One of our club members was a student with you at the Tenth of
November Institute of Technology and also went to Malang. He
currently drives a septic truck. Another club member said you
marched him around in the military. He liked it. If you like you
could be the head of our dessert club. Consider it. Post will be
open until 3/12/2010. Then Agus Gunter will probably get it or
maybe Floyd Meeb. They both like writing poems. One of our
members said you had a volleyball club called Klub Rajawali. It
is a small peaceful world.

There is a very nice picture of you i have eating custard or
Yogurt or some Indonesian goo. May I show it to others?

Thank you for you reply. Keep up the good work.

PLEASE SEND ME AN AUTOGRAPHED PICTURE. I will show it to my
Indonesian club . (then put it away)

With utter respect,

F.D. Nooey

F.D. Nancy (MR)

SEKRETARIAT NEGARA RI
RUMAH TANGGA KEPRESIDENAN

Jakarta, 11 January 2010

Mr. F.D. Nancy
1413 1 / 2 Kenneth Rd. #193
Glendale, CA 91201
USA

Dear Mr. Nancy,

As requested I am pleased to send herewith a photograph of the President of the Republic of Indonesia, H.E. Dr. Susilo Bambang Yudhoyono.

Wishing you every success.

Head of Administration Bureau
Presidential Household,

Sarosari Sulistyo

SEKRETARIAT NEGARA RI
RUMAH TANGGA KEPRESIDENAN

R **POSTAGE PAID**
International Registered
Bea Kirim Rp
RR 00089977 9 ID   A

RR 00089977 9 ID   B

Mr. F.D. Nancy
1413 ½ Kenneth Rd. # 193
Glendale, CA 91201
USA

Btk.S.1.4.

Family eating goo →

YUDHOYONO AIRPORT PLATE GLASS WINDOWS
"ONLY BUSINESS SIZE PLATE GLASS WINDOWS
ONLY AT THE AIRPORT"

1413 1/2 Kenneth Rd. #193
Glendale, CA 91201
f.d.nancy@lycos.com

Leasing
Esbjerg Airport
John Tranumsvej 22
6705 Esbjerg E
info@esbjerg-lufthavn.dk   7/12/9

Dear Esbjerg Airport.:

I was told to write you about leasing space at your airport in
Denmark for my business: YUDHOYONO AIRPORT PLATE GLASS WINDOWS

I sell plate glass windows 6 feet high by 12 feet long. Only at
the Airport. We keep our prices low because it's strictly self
service. These are Business Size Windows, Bank Glass, coffee shop
piece of glass.

We have no employees to keep prices down. Sure you may pay more
because you bought it at the Airport but you pay less because we
have no help, deliveries, overhead (except airport rental)

Simply visit our store - select your large sheet of plate glass -
get it from the top shelf - take it down - bring it to the
register - and pay for it. It's as easy at that. YUDHOYONO
AIRPORT PLATE GLASS WINDOWS are easy to maneuver in large crowds
and tight spaces. Take it on the plane.

I want to open in your airport. Can you tell em how I can lease
airport space from you for my business. I may also need people to
work for me. Can you assist me in getting some workers?

Sincerely,

F.D. Nancy

244

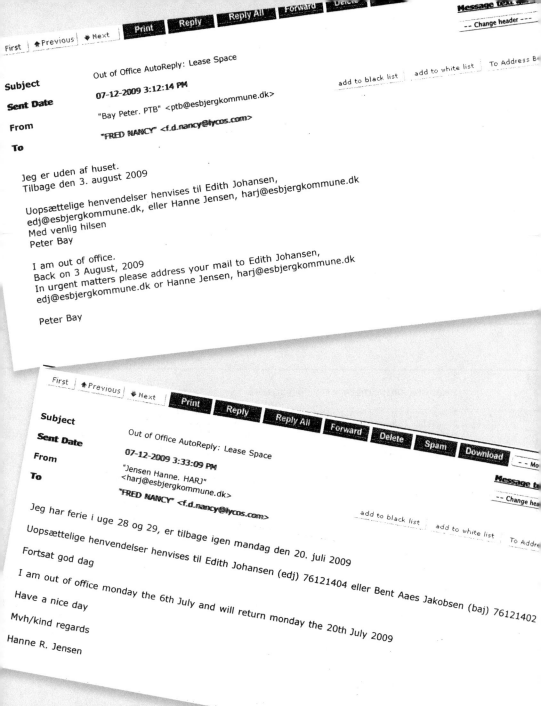

-- Change header ---

Subject
Out of Office AutoReply: Lease Space

Sent Date
07-12-2009 3:12:14 PM

From
"Bay Peter. PTB" <ptb@esbjergkommune.dk>

To
"FRED NANCY" <f.d.nancy@lycos.com>

add to black list   add to white list   To Address B

Jeg er uden af huset.
Tilbage den 3. august 2009

Uopsættelige henvendelser henvises til Edith Johansen,
edj@esbjergkommune.dk, eller Hanne Jensen, harj@esbjergkommune.dk
Med venlig hilsen
Peter Bay

I am out of office.
Back on 3 August, 2009
In urgent matters please address your mail to Edith Johansen,
edj@esbjergkommune.dk or Hanne Jensen, harj@esbjergkommune.dk

Peter Bay

Subject
Out of Office AutoReply: Lease Space

Sent Date
07-12-2009 3:33:09 PM

From
"Jensen Hanne. HARJ"
<harj@esbjergkommune.dk>

To
"FRED NANCY" <f.d.nancy@lycos.com>

add to black list   add to white list   To Addre

Jeg har ferie i uge 28 og 29, er tilbage igen mandag den 20. juli 2009

Uopsættelige henvendelser henvises til Edith Johansen (edj) 76121404 eller Bent Aaes Jakobsen (baj) 76121402

Fortsat god dag

I am out of office monday the 6th July and will return monday the 20th July 2009

Have a nice day

Mvh/kind regards

Hanne R. Jensen

1413 1/2 Kenneth Rd. #193
Glendale, CA 91201

Donations Dept.
The University of South Dakota Business Office
414 East Clark St.
207 Slagle Hall
Vermillion, SD 57069   July 6, 2009

Dear The University of South Dakota :

I am writing to your fine college today with great honor for me.
I would like to leave a donation to The University of South
Dakota . Pierre holds a lot of fond memories and your school has
educated many. I have had 12 of your former students working for
me at various times.

I would like to now leave a donation to you. We are doing well.
Your past students have helped our business become what it is
today.

Who do I contact to leave my gift? Can you advise me? I am
honored to be able to do this. I look forward to your reply.

Sincerely,

F.D. Nancy

F.D. Nancy (MR)

U.

The **U**niversity of South Dakota.

FOUNDATION

July 14, 2009

Mr. F.D. Nancy
1413 1/2 Kenneth Road
#193
Glendale, CA 91201

Dear Mr. Nancy,

How wonderful to receive your letter. We are pleased you had a good experience employing our graduates. We are proud of the young men and women who leave our campus and make this world a better place.

Your letter was received by the University of South Dakota. It was forwarded to me at the USD Foundation because the USD Foundation is the entity that accepts gifts on behalf of the University. I am the Director of Planned Giving at the USD Foundation, and you may contact me. I will be happy to advise or help you as you wish to make this gift.

Below I have listed our telephone numbers, our address, and the Tax ID Number for the USD Foundation. I am also enclosing a photograph of Old Main, the oldest academic building on campus. It was restored about 12 years ago and is a stunning classroom building.

I look forward to further communication with you.

Most sincerely,

Susan L. Tuve
Director of Planned Giving

Toll Free: 800-521-3575
Direct: 605-677-5527
Address: USD Foundation
          PO Box 5555
          Vermillion, SD 57069
USD Foundation Tax ID # 46-6018891

Enclosure

1413 1/2 Kenneth Rd. #193
Glendale, CA 91201

MS Susan Tuve
The University of South Dakota
USD Foundation PO Box 5555
Vermillion, SD 57069   Aug 21, 2009

Dear MS Tuve.

My name is Ted L. Nancy. F.D. Nancy (Fred) sent me a postcard.
He is vacationing. He snorkeled. Threw a dart. He has a rash.
He likes where he is at. He ripped his bathing suit. He still
has a gift for you.

Sincerely,

Ted L. Nancy
Ted L. Nancy

POST CARD

My Room

Hey Jed, it's me Fred.
Having a great time.
Snorkeling, darts, wrestled
a raccoon. Its name was
Roy. I have a rash. The
Place where I'm at is
great! Its an red
building with a lot of
windows. My shoelace
broke. Let univ. I SD know
I still have a gift for them.
my elastic gave out. Be home
soon. F.D.

POST CARD

ADDRESS

Jed L. Nancy
1413 1/2 Kenneth Rd.
#193
Glendale, CA 90201

epilogue

1413 1/2 Kenneth Rd. #193
Glendale, CA 91201

Lost & Found
Ritz Carlton Hotel
Suzer Plaza, Elmadag
Askerocagi Cad. No: 15
34367 Sisli - Istanbul
Turkey   14 May 2009

Dear Ritz Carlton Hotel Turkey:

I am wondering if you found a RUBBER GORILLA CHEST WITH RUBBER
GORILLA NIPPLES on it. I lost them in your hotel. Let me
describe: these are nipples approximately 1 inch long by 1/2 inch
around. They do not squirt; rubber, not real. Only one has an
indent in it. May have a hair. The chest looks like any chest
(on a gorilla) Did you find? It may have loosened in the
bathroom when I took off my rubber gorilla feet?

I was distracted when I needed a wipette and you were out. so I
went to another stall to get a moist towelette and to see if you
had a sanitary protective guard. With both stalls open, a mirror
in my eyes, and disoriented I became confused and foggy. ROY!

Did you find? This rubber gorilla chest has no value other then
to me for presentations. It is hairy. Maybe someone turned it
in. Maybe they took it to the restaurant. It is someplace.
Where?

You are a fine hotel.   And most courteous to your guests.

Restfully,

F.D. Nancy
F.D. Nancy (MR)

P.S. You have great Kebabs!

THE RITZ-CARLTON®
ISTANBUL

May 25, 2009

F.D. Nancy (MR)

1413 ½ Kenneth Rd. #193
Glendale, CA 91201

Dear Mr. Nancy,

I would like to kindly inform you that thru all the investigations we have done in the
restaurant and lobby area (including the mens restroom) we could not find your lost
item. We have also looked thru our records, but no item similar as you are mentioning
has been delivered to our department.
For your kind information.

Kind Regards,

Mehmet DURMUS
Loss & Prevention Manager

Süzer Plaza, Elmadağ, 34367 Şişli, İstanbul Turkey
Tel: +90 (212) 334 44 44 - Fax: +90 (212) 334 44 55

ACKNOWLEDGMENTS

Dan Strone of Trident Media Group and his assistant, Lyuba DiFalco. Charlie Conrad and Jenna Ciongoli of Broadway Books. Alan Marder, Susan Marder, Cookie and Mark Silver, Sharon Siegel, Justin Siegel, Nancy Abrams, Marilyn, Cele, and Marty. Dan Halsted, Nate Miller and Hershel Davis in Dan's office, Hershel Pearl, and Johnny Dark. Jose at the mail place. Dr. Mickey Weisberg, Jeanne. Dr. Mark Gerard, Irma, Mel, and Anna, who take care of Me. Dr. Michael Robbins, Jessica, Vicki, Nataliya, Roksana—Tooth. Dr. Douglas Shreck—Heart. Dr. Curtis Howard—Back. Dr. Jenna Libed—Toe. Dr. Theodore Goldstein—Spine. Eric Bjorgum, lawyer to me, Ted L. Nancy. Settled tartar sauce suit with extreme crab fishermen. Keeps filth off me.

Linda Shaw, Deborah Gottlieb, Bill, Ann, and Connie Hunt, Jack and Kim Wiener, Larry Vazeos, Philip Halpern, Stanley, Dollie, Andy, Ivan, Betsy Jonas, Alyson Daar, and Brody and Annie.

Phyllis Murphy. Who puts up with me. I know I wouldn't do it. But that's just me. I tell her, "I'm easy like Sunday morning. That's because I'm on medication Saturday night." Ted is in love with her.

And a special thanks to Jerry Seinfeld, who gives far more than he ever receives. If only everybody knew.

ABOUT THE AUTHOR

Ted L. Nancy is a proud citizen of the United States of America. He is a veteran, having served in the United States Air Force for four years. (Truth.) He does not like chives. He will tolerate pimentos in his tuna. He has moved to Glendale, California, to be closer to the Turkish paranormal community. He has made contact and has been examined aboard a UFO. (But it could have been an apartment in Reno. All he knows is someone yelled, "Dude," and held his shirt up, and he saw IKEA shelving.)

Write to him at:

Ted L. Nancy
1413 1/2 Kenneth Rd. #193
Glendale, CA 91201

Visit him at: TedLNancy.com